GRAPHIS   MUSIC   CD   1

GRAPHIS MUSIC CD 1

. . . .

AN INTERNATIONAL COLLECTION OF CD DESIGN

CD-DESIGN IM INTERNATIONALEN ÜBERBLICK

UNE COMPILATION INTERNATIONALE SUR LE DESIGN DES CD

EDITED BY • HERAUSGEGEBEN VON • EDITÉ PAR:

B. MARTIN PEDERSEN

PUBLISHER AND CREATIVE DIRECTOR: B. MARTIN PEDERSEN

EDITORS: ANNETTE CRANDALL, HEINKE JENSSEN

ASSISTANT EDITORS: VALERIE ARNADE, JÖRG REIMANN

ART DIRECTORS: B. MARTIN PEDERSEN, RANDELL PEARSON

PHOTOGRAPHERS: ALFREDO PARRAGA, WALTER ZUBER

GRAPHIS PRESS CORP. ZÜRICH (SWITZERLAND)

CONTENTS · INHALT · SOMMAIRE

REMARKS

WE EXTEND OUR HEARTFELT THANKS TO CONTRIBUTORS THROUGHOUT THE WORLD WHO HAVE MADE IT POSSIBLE TO PUBLISH A WIDE AND INTERNATIONAL SPECTRUM OF THE BEST WORK IN THIS FIELD.

ENTRY INSTRUCTIONS FOR THE NEXT BOOK ON CD DESIGN MAY BE REQUESTED AT:
GRAPHIS PRESS
141 LEXINGTON AVENUE
NEW YORK, NY 10016-8193

ANMERKUNGEN

UNSER DANK GILT DEN EINSENDERN AUS ALLER WELT, DIE ES UNS DURCH IHRE BEI-TRÄGE ERMÖGLICHT HABEN, EIN BREITES, INTERNATIONALES SPEKTRUM DER BESTEN ARBEITEN ZU VERÖFFENTLICHEN.

TEILNAHMEBEDINGUNGEN FÜR DAS NÄCHSTE BUCH ÜBER CD-DESIGN SIND ERHÄLTLICH BEIM:
GRAPHIS VERLAG AG
DUFOURSTRASSE 107
8008 ZÜRICH, SCHWEIZ

REMERCIEMENTS

NOUS REMERCIONS LES PARTICIPANTS DU MONDE ENTIER QUI ONT RENDU POSSIBLE LA PUBLICATION DE CET OUVRAGE OFFRANT UN PANORAMA COMPLET DES MEILLEURS TRA-VAUX RÉALISÉS DANS CE DOMAINE.

LES MODALITÉS D'INSCRIPTION PEUVENT ÊTRE OBTENUES AUPRÈS DE:
EDITIONS GRAPHIS
DUFOURSTRASSE 107
8008 ZÜRICH, SUISSE

(PRECEDING SPREAD) ART DIRECTOR: AL CONNOR PHOTOGRAPHER: PAUL ARESU

■ (OPPOSITE) RECORD COMPANY: WINDHAM HILL ART DIRECTOR: JENNIFER MORLA DESIGNERS: JENNIFER MORLA, JEANETTE ARAMBURU

PHOTOGRAPHER: GERRY BYBEE DESIGN FIRM: MORLA DESIGN PERFORMING ARTIST: TUCK & PATTI ALBUM TITLE: DREAM

GRAPHIS PUBLICATIONS

GRAPHIS, THE INTERNATIONAL BI-MONTHLY JOURNAL OF VISUAL COMMUNICATION

GRAPHIS DESIGN, THE INTERNATIONAL ANNUAL OF DESIGN AND ILLUSTRATION

GRAPHIS ADVERTISING, THE INTERNATIONAL ANNUAL OF ADVERTISING

GRAPHIS BROCHURES, A COMPILATION OF BROCHURE DESIGN

GRAPHIS PHOTO, THE INTERNATIONAL ANNUAL OF PHOTOGRAPHY

GRAPHIS ALTERNATIVE PHOTOGRAPHY, THE INTERNATIONAL ANNUAL OF ALTERNATIVE PHOTOGRAPHY

GRAPHIS NUDES, A COLLECTION OF CAREFULLY SELECTED SOPHISTICATED IMAGES

GRAPHIS POSTER, THE INTERNATIONAL ANNUAL OF POSTER ART

GRAPHIS PACKAGING, AN INTERNATIONAL COMPILATION OF PACKAGING DESIGN

GRAPHIS LETTERHEAD, AN INTERNATIONAL COMPILATION OF LETTERHEAD DESIGN

GRAPHIS DIAGRAM, THE GRAPHIC VISUALIZATION OF ABSTRACT, TECHNICAL AND STATISTICAL FACTS AND FUNCTIONS

GRAPHIS LOGO, AN INTERNATIONAL COMPILATION OF LOGOS

GRAPHIS EPHEMERA, AN INTERNATIONAL COLLECTION OF PROMOTIONAL ART

GRAPHIS PUBLICATION, AN INTERNATIONAL SURVEY OF THE BEST IN MAGAZINE DESIGN

GRAPHIS ANNUAL REPORTS, AN INTERNATIONAL COMPILATION OF THE BEST DESIGNED ANNUAL REPORTS

GRAPHIS CORPORATE IDENTITY, AN INTERNATIONAL COMPILATION OF THE BEST IN CORPORATE IDENTITY DESIGN

GRAPHIS TYPOGRAPHY, AN INTERNATIONAL COMPILATION OF THE BEST IN TYPOGRAPHIC DESIGN

ART FOR SURVIVAL: THE ILLUSTRATOR AND THE ENVIRONMENT, A DOCUMENT OF ART IN THE SERVICE OF MAN.

THE GRAPHIC DESIGNER'S GREEN BOOK, ENVIRONMENTAL RESOURCES FOR THE DESIGN AND PRINT INDUSTRIES

GRAPHIS PUBLIKATIONEN

GRAPHIS, DIE INTERNATIONALE ZWEIMONATSZEITSCHRIFT DER VISUELLEN KOMMUNIKATION

GRAPHIS DESIGN, DAS INTERNATIONALE JAHRBUCH ÜBER DESIGN UND ILLUSTRATION

GRAPHIS ADVERTISING, DAS INTERNATIONALE JAHRBUCH DER WERBUNG

GRAPHIS BROCHURES, BROSCHÜRENDESIGN IM INTERNATIONAL ÜBERBLICK

GRAPHIS PHOTO, DAS INTERNATIONALE JAHRBUCH DER PHOTOGRAPHIE

GRAPHIS ALTERNATIVE PHOTOGRAPHY, DAS INTERNATIONALE JAHRBUCH ÜBER ALTERNATIVE PHOTOGRAPHIE

GRAPHIS NUDES, EINE SAMMLUNG SORGFÄLTIG AUSGEWÄHLTER AKTPHOTOGRAPHIE

GRAPHIS POSTER, DAS INTERNATIONALE JAHRBUCH DER PLAKATKUNST

GRAPHIS PACKAGING, EIN INTERNATIONALER ÜBERBLICK ÜBER DIE PACKUNGSGESTALTUNG

GRAPHIS LETTERHEAD, EIN INTERNATIONALER ÜBERBLICK ÜBER BRIEFPAPIERGESTALTUNG

GRAPHIS DIAGRAM, DIE GRAPHISCHE DARSTELLUNG ABSTRAKTER TECHNISCHER UND STATISTISCHER DATEN UND FAKTEN

GRAPHIS LOGO, EINE INTERNATIONALE AUSWAHL VON FIRMEN-LOGOS

GRAPHIS EPHEMERA, EINE INTERNATIONALE SAMMLUNG GRAPHISCHER DOKUMENTE DES TÄGLICHEN LEBENS

GRAPHIS MAGAZINDESIGN, EINE INTERNATIONALE ZUSAMMENSTELLUNG DES BESTEN ZEITSCHRIFTEN-DESIGNS

GRAPHIS ANNUAL REPORTS, EIN INTERNATIONALER ÜBERBLICK ÜBER DIE GESTALTUNG VON JAHRESBERICHTEN

GRAPHIS CORPORATE IDENTITY, EINE INTERNATIONALE AUSWAHL DES BESTEN CORPORATE IDENTITY DESIGNS

GRAPHIS TYPOGRAPHY, EINE INTERNATIONALE ZUSAMMENSTELLUNG DES BESTEN TYPOGRAPHIE DESIGN

ART FOR SURVIVAL: THE ILLUSTRATOR AND THE ENVIRONMENT, EIN DOKUMENT ÜBER DIE KUNST IM DIENSTE DES MENSCHEN

THE GRAPHIC DESIGNER'S GREEN BOOK, UMWELTKONZEPTE DER DESIGN- UND DRUCKINDUSTRIE

PUBLICATIONS GRAPHIS

GRAPHIS, LA REVUE BIMESTRIELLE INTERNATIONALE DE LA COMMUNICATION VISUELLE

GRAPHIS DESIGN, LE RÉPERTOIRE INTERNATIONAL DE LA COMMUNICATION VISUELLE

GRAPHIS ADVERTISING, LE RÉPERTOIRE INTERNATIONAL DE LA PUBLICITÉ

GRAPHIS BROCHURES, UNE COMPILATION INTERNATIONALE SUR LE DESIGN DES BROCHURES

GRAPHIS PHOTO, LE RÉPERTOIRE INTERNATIONAL DE LA PHOTOGRAPHIE

GRAPHIS ALTERNATIVE PHOTOGRAPHY, LE RÉPERTOIRE INTERNATIONAL DE LA PHOTOGRAPHIE ALTERNATIVE

GRAPHIS NUDES, UN FLORILÈGE DE LA PHOTOGRAPHIE DE NUS

GRAPHIS POSTER, LE RÉPERTOIRE INTERNATIONAL DE L'AFFICHE

GRAPHIS PACKAGING, LE RÉPERTOIRE INTERNATIONAL DE LA CRÉATION D'EMBALLAGES

GRAPHIS LETTERHEAD, LE RÉPERTOIRE INTERNATIONAL DU DESIGN DE PAPIER À LETTRES

GRAPHIS DIAGRAM, LE RÉPERTOIRE GRAPHIQUE DE FAITS ET DONNÉES ABSTRAITS, TECHNIQUES ET STATISTIQUES

GRAPHIS LOGO, LE RÉPERTOIRE INTERNATIONAL DU LOGO

GRAPHIS EPHEMERA, LE GRAPHISME – UN ÉTAT D'ESPRIT AU QUOTIDIEN

GRAPHIS PUBLICATION, LE RÉPERTOIRE INTERNATIONAL DU DESIGN DE PÉRIODIQUES

GRAPHIS ANNUAL REPORTS, PANORAMA INTERNATIONAL DU MEILLEUR DESIGN DE RAPPORTS ANNUELS D'ENTREPRISES

GRAPHIS CORPORATE IDENTITY, PANORAMA INTERNATIONAL DU MEILLEUR DESIGN D'IDENTITÉ CORPORATE

GRAPHIS TYPOGRAPHY, LE RÉPERTOIRE INTERNATIONAL DU MEILLEUR DESIGN DE TYPOGRAPHIE

ART FOR SURVIVAL: THE ILLUSTRATOR AND THE ENVIRONMENT, L'ART AU SERVICE DE LA SURVIE

THE GRAPHIC DESIGNER'S GREEN BOOK, L'ÉCOLOGIE APPLIQUÉE AU DESIGN ET À L'INDUSTRIE GRAPHIQUE

PUBLICATION NO. 245 (ISBN 3-85709-459-1)

© COPYRIGHT UNDER UNIVERSAL COPYRIGHT CONVENTION

COPYRIGHT © 1995 BY GRAPHIS PRESS CORP., DUFOURSTRASSE 107, 8008 ZURICH, SWITZERLAND

JACKET AND BOOK DESIGN COPYRIGHT © 1995 BY PEDERSEN DESIGN

141 LEXINGTON AVENUE, NEW YORK, N.Y. 10016 USA

PRINTED BY PALACE PRESS INTERNATIONAL, HONG KONG/NEW YORK

COMMENTARY

KOMMENTAR

COMMENTAIRE

Robin Sloane

Unlike most people in my profession, I am not a trained graphic designer. I did not graduate from art school. I arrived at my position purely because I have always been in love with records. My years of working inside the music business led to my current position as creative director of Geffen Records. In this role, I oversee all visual production for the artists and the company, including album packaging, print and TV advertising, retail merchandising and music video production. □ Because my ascent was not through the ranks in the design profession, I probably have a different perspective on the current and future state of CD design than others in my field. There are days when I feel like Tom Hanks in the movie *Big*. I recall my own memories as a kid in a record store, or at home wearing headphones and staring at album covers, asking myself: What makes one cover draw me in more than others? The answer remains the same—a good idea. □ In the early years of my career, I worked on artists' images via music videos. From this I learned a key factor: An artist's image should translate into many different media. □ I believe in creating complete visual campaigns for which the packaging and music video must be the cornerstone. All the visual elements should be true to each other, though not necessarily identical throughout the various media. The concerns of the visual artists cannot exclude the music artist. My aim is to tie the musician in with the designer, video director, and advertising and merchandising departments. □ It's imperative to create an image that can be carried through all forms of print and TV media, rather than just the CD cover. It must be strong enough to catch a consumer's eye and immediately connect with some emotion. In creating an interpretation on film, the video director must be able to understand the reasons why specific images were chosen and the rationale behind the creative direction of the overall campaign. □ A designer's versatility is essential. We've failed when a specific designer's style dominates the package. The job of the designer is to use his or her skills to translate the music into a visual media. Designers must put their egos aside and concentrate on the music and development of the artist's image. Music is an emotional experience and the artist is a living being—these are the elements to be communicated, rather than the design itself. The musician is the primary artist, not the designer. □ Two recent projects demonstrate this thought process: Counting Crows' *August and Everything After* and Nelson's *Because They Can*. At the time of *August and Everything After*, Counting Crows were a brand new band with a strong and charismatic writer and lead singer. They had never released any records before and were new to the entire visual process. We searched for months, with no success, for an appropriate image to communicate the artist's evocative lyrical imagery. In thinking through our problems, I realized that this album is about words; the power of the music rests in the songwriter's use of lyrics. We decided to create the campaign around these words and actually used a page out of the artist's handwritten song journal as the cover image. We carried this through into our advertising and merchandising. Meanwhile, the video director created a video which relied on the artist's expressive interpretation of the song combined with a visually lyrical interpretation of differing scenarios with actors portraying the words. The approach worked. A year after release, the album had sold more than 4 million copies throughout the world. □ With Nelson, we were dealing with the second album from a band led by the identical twin sons of the hugely successful pop star Ricky Nelson; the grandsons of Ozzy and Harriet Nelson. They had a multi-million selling debut album which traded on a glitzy, pop image built largely around the long platinum-blond hair for which they had become renowned. This kind of image in the music world is often transitory and is also difficult to move beyond. With Nelson's new record, their music had grown, having been toned down to a more acoustic sound relying on melodic harmonies. How do we get that sense of change across to an audience who had aged several years, possibly thinking back to this group with a bit of cynicism? The artists' intention with the album was to harken back to their roots, a Southern California style of music, and they were ready to poke some fun at their previous image. What could be a more perfect cover than William Wegman's dogs with blond wigs parodying the Nelson twins' long blond hair? We finally convinced Wegman to do the shoot, provided that he had free reign to interpret it the way he wanted. How could we go wrong? So we packed up two wigs rented and styled in L.A., the Nelsons' old clothes and guitars, and crossed our fingers. The result couldn't be more appropriate for the campaign. The album was released in the summer of 1995. □ Designers must realize what we are selling—these are not man-made products, they are human beings. We must visually interpret the artist's goals and motivations and capture them without compromising the artist's ethics—and still meet the company's marketing needs. □ As far as I can see, the field is getting better. Those of us who drew our inspirations from album covers are finally coming to terms with the much smaller palette we now have to work with. Those just now joining the field aren't carrying LP-cover baggage along with them. The 5x5-inch size of CDs, and the even smaller cassette format, demand different visual solutions. □ We continue to face a host of technical issues, from the future of the plastic jewel box to the feasibility of recyclable cardboard jackets, to the optimum use of computer-generated designs versus more old-fashioned and manual techniques, to typographic treatments and stock choices. I'm fortunate enough to be able to work with many extremely talented designers and music artists. The musicians and their image concerns are paramount. They're the ones who bring us the chance to do what we do, and who give life to all our work. They're the ones that allow me to remain the kid with the headphones on trying to figure out what makes one cover better than the other. □ One last thought: It's too bad a hardware manufacturer hasn't designed a translucent CD player. One of the most overlooked areas of CD design has become the disc itself. I think this is where designers must have the most fun, because it's always exciting to see some new way of using the disc itself in the overall packaging design. It's a shame they can't be seen the way vinyl was, instead of the whole design being swallowed up inside the CD player. Maybe we can present this challenge to the hardware designers of the future. ∎

ROBIN SLOANE IS THE CREATIVE DIRECTOR OF GEFFEN RECORDS

Im Gegensatz zu den meisten meiner Berufskollegen bin ich nicht ausgebildete Graphik-Designerin. Ich habe keine Kunstschule besucht. Ich habe meine Stellung bekommen, weil Schallplatten schon immer meine grosse Liebe waren. Ich habe jahrelang Erfahrungen in der Musikbranche gesammelt, bevor ich Creative Director von Geffen Records wurde. Ich überwache heute sämtliche visuellen Produktionen für die Künstler und die Firma, einschliesslich der Verpackung der Musikerzeugnisse, Druck- und TV-Werbung, Verkaufshilfen für den Einzelhandel und die Produktion von Musik-Videos. ◻ Da ich nicht vom Design herkomme, habe ich von der heutigen und zukünftigen Gestaltung von CDs wahrscheinlich eine ganz andere Vorstellung als die meisten meiner Kollegen. Ich erinnere mich, was ich als Kind in einem Plattenladen empfunden habe oder was mir durch den Kopf ging, als ich zuhause, Kopfhörer aufgesetzt, die Plattenhüllen betrachtete: Warum zieht mich eine bestimmte Hülle mehr an als andere? Die Antwort lautet noch immer gleich: der Unterschied liegt in der guten Idee. ◻ Zu Beginn meiner Laufbahn befasste ich mich mit dem Image der Künstler via Musikvideos. Dabei lernte ich etwas ganz Wesentliches: Das Image eines Künstlers sollte sich in vielen verschiedenen Medien ausdrücken lassen. ◻ Für mich müssen visuelle Kampagnen alles einschliessen, wobei die Verpackung und das Musikvideo die Eckpfeiler bilden. Alle visuellen Elemente müssen aufeinander abgestimmt, aber in den verschiedenen Medien nicht unbedingt identisch sein. Der visuelle Künstler kann bei seinen Überlegungen den Musikkünstler nicht ausschliessen. Deshalb lege ich Wert darauf, den Musiker mit dem Designer, Video-Regisseur sowie mit den Werbe- und Merchandisingabteilungen zusammenzubringen. ◻ Ein Image muss sich, wie gesagt, in Print-und TV-Medien ebenso gut umsetzen lassen wie bei der CD-Hülle. Es muss stark genug sein, um die Aufmerksamkeit des Konsumenten zu erregen und bestimmte Empfindungen wachzurufen. Bei der Umsetzung für ein Video muss der Regisseur verstehen, warum gewisse Bilder gewählt wurden, er muss die der gesamten Kampagne zugrundeliegenden Gedankengänge kennen. ◻ Ganz wichtig ist auch die Flexibilität eines Designers. Wenn der Stil des Designers die Hülle der CD prägt, haben wir versagt. Seine Aufgabe ist es, sein Können einzusetzen, um die Musik in ein visuelles Medium zu übertragen. Dabei muss er sein Ego vergessen und sich auf die Musik und das Image des Künstlers konzentrieren. Musik ist eine emotionale Erfahrung, und der Künstler ist ein lebendiges Wesen – nur das zählt, nicht das Design als solches. Der Musiker ist der Künstler, um den es geht, nicht der Designer. ◻ Zwei kürzliche Projekte verdeutlichen diesen Denkprozess: *August and Everything After* von den Counting Crows und *Because They Can* von den Nelsons. Als sie *August und Everything After* aufnahmen, waren die Counting Crows eine neue Band mit einem starken, charismatischen Texter und Leadsänger. Sie hatten noch nie eine Platte herausgebracht, und der gesamte visuelle Prozess war völlig neu für sie. Wir suchten monatelang vergeblich nach einem passenden Image, das den evokativen Texten gerecht werden würde. Als ich über unsere Probleme nachdachte, wurde mir klar, dass es bei diesem Album um Worte ging; die Musik schöpft ihre Kraft aus den Texten. Wir beschlossen, die Kampagne auf diesen Worten aufzubauen und verwendeten eine Seite aus dem handgeschriebenen Songbuch als Cover. Dieses Thema zogen wir durch unsere gesamte Werbung und das Merchandising. Unterdessen arbeitete der Regisseur an einem Video, das sich auf die ausdrucksvolle Interpretation der Songs stützte und sehr lyrische Bilder enthielt, wobei Schauspieler in verschiedenen Szenarios die Worte interpretierten. Das Konzept war erfolgreich. Ein Jahr nach seinem Erscheinen waren bereits weltweit 4 Millionen Stück des Albums verkauft. ◻ Bei den Nelsons ging es um das zweite Album der Band, die von den Zwillingssöhnen des sehr erfolgreichen Pop Stars Ricky Nelson angeführt wird; es sind die Enkel von Ozzy und Harriet Nelson. Bei ihrem ersten Album, von dem mehrere Millionen verkauft wurden, wurden sie als glamouröse Popstars präsentiert, wobei ihr langes, platinblondes Haar, quasi ihr Markenzeichen, das Thema war. Diese Art von Image in der Musik ist oft nicht sehr langlebig, andererseits ist es ungeheuer schwer, davon loszukommen. Die zweite Platte zeigte, dass sich die Musik der Nelsons weiterentwickelt hatte, sie klang weniger elektronisch, enthielt melodische Harmonien. Wie sollten wir dem Publikum diese Entwicklung verdeutlichen, einem Publikum, das inzwischen einige Jahre älter geworden war und vielleicht jetzt hinsichtlich des bisherigen Images der Gruppe gemischte Gefühle hatte. Bei diesem Album besannen sich die Musiker auf ihre Wurzeln, eine südkalifornische Musik. Sie waren bereit, sich über ihr bisheriges Image ein bisschen lustig zu machen. Was hätte sich dafür besser geeignet als William Wegmans Hunde mit blonden Perücken – eine Parodie auf das lange Haar der Nelson-Zwillinge? Wegman war bereit, die Aufnahmen zu machen, unter der Bedingung, dass er in seiner Interpretation völlig frei sein würde. Wir besorgten also zwei Perücken, die in Los Angeles hergerichtet wurden, die alten Kleider und Gitarren der Nelsons und drückten die Daumen. Das Ergebnis hätte für die Kampagne nicht besser sein können. Das Album ist im Sommer 1995 herausgekommen. ◻ Designer müssen sich klar darüber sein, was wir verkaufen: Es geht nicht um Produkte, es geht um Menschen. Wir müssen die Ziele und Motivationen der Künstler visuell umsetzen, ihnen gerecht werden und trotzdem auch die für die Firma wichtigen Marketing-Aspekte berücksichtigen. ◻ Soweit ich es beurteilen kann, werden Fortschritte gemacht. All jene von uns, die sich einst von den LP-Hüllen inspirieren liessen, haben sich schliesslich an das viel kleinere Format, mit dem wir jetzt zurechtkommen müssen, gewöhnt. Die Neulinge in unserer Branche tragen die Altlast der grossen LP-Hüllen nicht mit sich herum. Die 5x5-Inch-grossen CDs und das noch kleinere Format der Tonbandkassetten verlangen nach anderen visuellen Lösungen. ◻ Immer wieder stehen wir vor technischen Fragen, ob es um die Fragen 'einfache Plastikhüllen oder wiederverwertbare Kartonhüllen' geht, 'Computer oder herkömmliche manuelle Techniken' oder um die Wahl der Typographie und des Papiers. Zum Glück arbeite ich mit vielen sehr talentierten Designern und Musikern zusammen. Die Musiker und ihr Image sind ungeheuer wichtig. Sie geben uns die Chance, das zu tun, was wir tun, und sie bringen Leben in unsere Arbeit. ◻ Ein letzter Gedanke: Es ist schade, dass noch kein Hersteller darauf gekommen ist, einen transparenten CD-Spieler zu entwerfen. Einer der am meisten vernachlässigten Bereiche des CD-Designs ist zweifellos die Diskette selbst. Ich meine, ihre Gestaltung macht den Designern am meisten Spass, weil es immer spannend ist, auf wie viele verschiedene Arten man die Diskette selbst als Element der Verpackung einsetzen kann. Es ist jammerschade, dass man sie nicht so wie seinerzeit die LPs sehen kann, weil der CD-Spieler sie einfach verschluckt. Vielleicht nehmen die zukünftigen Designer der CD-Spieler diese Herausforderung an. ∎

ROBIN SLOANE IST KREATIVDIREKTORIN BEI GEFFEN RECORDS

Contrairement à la plupart des professionnels de ma branche, je ne suis pas graphiste et je ne suis pas diplômée d'une école d'art. Si l'on m'a confié la direction artistique de Greffen Records, c'est uniquement parce que j'ai toujours aimé les disques. Mes années d'expérience dans l'édition de disques m'ont amenée à assumer la supervision de toute la production visuelle de la maison de disques, des pochettes à la publicité imprimée et télévisuelle, en passant par la promotion au point de vente et la production de vidéos musicales. □ Etant donné que je suis venue à la profession de manière indirecte, ma perspective sur l'évolution présente et future du design des disques compacts est sans doute différente de celle de mes collègues. Il y a des jours où je me sens comme Tom Hanks dans le film *Big*. Je me rappelle l'époque où enfant, je déambulais dans les magasins de disque et à la maison avec un casque sur les oreilles me demandant: «Qu'est-ce qui me fait préférer cette pochette à une autre?» La réponse est encore la même aujourd'hui: une bonne idée. □ Dans les premières années de ma carrière, j'ai travaillé sur l'image des vedettes dans les vidéos musicales. J'ai appris une chose importante: l'image d'un artiste doit pouvoir s'adapter à différents supports médiatiques. □ Je crois qu'il est nécessaire de créer des campagnes d'image globales, où le conditionnement et la vidéo servent de référence. Les divers éléments visuels doivent être complémentaires, quoique pas forcément identiques, dans les divers médias. Le professionnel de la communication visuelle ne peut cependant pas ignorer le musicien. Ma fonction est justement de servir de lien entre le musicien, le graphiste, le producteur de la vidéo ainsi que les départements de publicité et de promotion des ventes. □ Il est impératif de créer un design qui ne soit pas uniquement adapté à la pochette de disque mais puisse être transposé aux divers médias imprimés et télévisuels. Il doit être suffisamment fort pour accrocher l'oeil du consommateur et susciter certaines émotions. Lors de la réalisation de la vidéo, le producteur doit comprendre les raisons qui ont motivé le choix de telle ou telle image et le concept global de la campagne. □ La flexibilité du designer est également essentielle. Nous avons échoué lorsque le graphiste imprimait à la pochette un style trop personnel. Un designer doit savoir mettre son talent au service de la visualisation de l'expression musicale. Il doit mettre son ego de côté et se concentrer sur la musique et l'image de l'artiste. La musique est une expérience émotionnelle et l'artiste est un être vivant, voilà les éléments à communiquer. C'est le musicien qu'il s'agit de mettre en valeur et non le graphiste. □ Deux projets récents illustrent bien cette démarche: *August and Everything After* de Counting Crows et *Because They Can* des Nelson. A l'époque d'*August and Everything After*, Counting Crows était un tout jeune groupe avec un parolier doué et un chanteur charismatique. Ils n'avaient jamais fait de disque auparavant et la problématique visuelle leur était inconnue. Nous avons cherché en vain pendant des mois une image qui exprime le lyrisme évocateur des paroles. Finalement j'ai réalisé que cet album tenait avant tout sur les mots et que le pouvoir de cette musique résidait dans l'usage que le parolier faisait du langage. Nous avons alors décidé d'articuler la campagne autour des mots et avons même utilisé une page du carnet de composition du parolier pour illustrer la pochette. Ce thème a trouvé son prolongement dans la campagne de publicité et de promotion des ventes. Entre temps, le producteur de la vidéo a réalisé un film qui s'appuyait sur l'interprétation très expressive du chanteur alternant avec des scènes poétiques jouées par des acteurs. Le concept a bien passé. Une année après sa sortie, l'album s'était vendu en 4 millions d'exemplaires dans le monde. □ Avec les Nelson, il s'agissait du second album d'un groupe mené par les frères jumeaux, fils de la célèbre vedette pop Ricky Nelson et petits-fils d'Ozzy et Harriet Nelson. Leur premier album s'était vendu en plusieurs millions d'exemplaires et la campagne jouait sur l'image rutilante des deux vedettes dont le signe distinctif était la longue chevelure blond-platine. Ce type d'image est généralement éphémère dans le monde musical mais il est souvent difficile de s'en défaire. Dans le nouvel album, la musique avait évolué d'un son très électronique vers des harmonies plus mélodiques. Comment exprimer ce changement musical à un public qui lui aussi avait évolué et qui peut-être s'était distancé du groupe? L'intention des artistes avec leur second album était de retrouver leurs racines, un style de la Californie du sud et ils étaient prêts à se moquer un peu leur image précédente. Qu'y avait-il de plus approprié que de montrer les deux chiens de William Wegman coiffés de deux perruques blondes, parodiant les longues chevelures des frères jumeaux? William Wegman s'est laissé convaincre de faire la photo à condition qu'on lui laisse la liberté d'interprétation. Nous avons loué deux perruques à Los Angeles, réuni les vieux habits des Nelson et avons tenu nos pouces. Le résultat n'aurait pas pu être meilleur. L'album est sorti en été 1995. Les designers doivent comprendre qu'il s'agit de promouvoir des personnes et non un produit. Nous devons interpréter visuellement les objectifs et les motivations des artistes en respectant leur éthique, tout en atteignant les objectifs publicitaires de l'entreprise. □ Pour autant que je puisse en juger, les choses s'améliorent. Tous ceux d'entre nous qui s'étaient jusqu'ici laissés inspirer par les pochettes de disques se sont finalement habitués à travailler avec des dimensions beaucoup plus réduites. Le format 12x14cm des CD et celui encore plus réduit des cassettes nécessitent une approche graphique différente. Les jeunes qui débutent dans la profession n'ont pas ce problème. □ De nombreuses questions techniques continuent à se poser. Qu'il s'agisse du choix entre la pochette plastique et la pochette recyclable en carton, entre la technique informatique ou des techniques de production plus traditionnelles, jusqu'au type de caractère et au choix du papier. J'ai la chance de pouvoir travailler avec beaucoup de designers et d'artistes de grand talent. Ce qui compte le plus pour moi ce sont les musiciens et leur image. Ce sont eux qui nous permettent de réaliser nos projets et ce sont eux qui insufflent de la vie à notre travail. Il y en a également qui me permettent de retrouver l'enfant que j'étais, avec mes écouteurs sur les oreilles en train de me demander ce qui distinguait une pochette d'une autre. □ Une dernière réflexion: c'est bien dommage que les fabricants n'aient pas encore conçu de lecteurs transparents. L'un des aspects les plus négligés du CD reste le disque lui-même. La conception du disque est un travail amusant pour le designer, parcequ'il est toujours intéressant de réfléchir comment intégrer la disquette au concept de l'emballage. C'est bien dommage que le CD ne soit pas visible comme l'était le vinyle. Peut-être pourrions nous proposer cette idée aux fabricants et designers du futur. ■

ROBIN SLOANE EST LA DIRECTRICE CREATIVE DE GEFFEN RECORDS

(OPPOSITE TOP LEFT) RECORD COMPANY: PHILIPS CLASSICS PROD. ART DIRECTOR: GEORGE CRAMER ILLUSTRATOR: SILVAN STEENBRINK PERFORMING ARTISTS: BEAUX ARTS TRIO ALBUM TITLE: PIANO TRIOS ■ (OPPOSITE TOP RIGHT) RECORD COMPANY: PHILIPS CLASSICS PROD. ART DIRECTOR: GEORGE CRAMER ILLUSTRATOR: ERTE PERFORMING ARTIST: ORCHESTRE DE PARIS ALBUM TITLE: PARIS 1920 ■ (OPPOSITE CENTER LEFT) RECORD COMPANY: SONY MUSIC ART DIRECTOR/DESIGNER: RISA ZAITSCHEK PHOTOGRAPHER: JASON STANG PERFORMING ARTIST: EMANUEL AX ALBUM TITLE: HAYDN PIANO SONATAS ■ (OPPOSITE CENTER RIGHT) RECORD COMPANY: SONY MUSIC ART DIRECTOR:

JIM DEBARROS DESIGNER: JIM DEBARROS PHOTOGRAPHER: THEA SCHRECK PERFORMING ARTIST: CHORALSCHOLA OF THE NIEDER-ALTAICHER SCHOLAREN ALBUM TITLE: GREGORIAN CHANT ■ (OPPOSITE BOTTOM LEFT) RECORD COMPANY: PHILIPS CLASSICS PROD. ART DIRECTOR: GEORGE CRAMER DESIGNER: PAUL WIGGERS PHOTOGRAPHER: RICHARD HOLT PERFORMING ARTIST: ZOLTAN KOCSIS ALBUM TITLE: BELA BARTOK: WORKS FOR PIANO SOLO 2 ■ (OPPOSITE BOTTOM RIGHT) RECORD COMPANY: SONY ART DIRECTOR: ALLEN WEINBERG PHOTOGRAPHER: KAREN KUEHN PERFORMING ARTIST: YO-YO MA ALBUM TITLE: THE NEW YORK ALBUM ■ (ABOVE) RECORD COMPANY: DENON ART DIRECTOR: LUTZ MENZE DESIGNER: LUTZ MENZE COVERS: ANDREAS WENDLER PERFORMING ARTISTS: VARIOUS ALBUM TITLES: VARIOUS

(BELOW) RECORD COMPANY: INTERCORD TON GMBH ART DIRECTORS: SUSANNE WACKER, WOLFRAM SCHÄFFER DESIGNERS: SUSANNE WACKER, WOLFRAM SCHÄFFER ILLUSTRATOR: WOLFRAM SCHÄFFER DESIGN FIRM: DESIGN HOCH DREI PERFORMING ARTIST: DJ NICK ALBUM TITLE: WHITE CHRISTMAS – RAVE ■ (OPPOSITE PAGE) RECORD COMPANY: CDCARD™ COMPANY, COURTESY OF THE BRIDGEMAN ART

LIBRARY ■ (OPPOSITE TOP) FRONT COVER SHOWS A SECTION OF "L'INNOCENCE" BY WILLIAM ADOLPH BOUGUEREAU (1825–1905) FROM CHRISTIE'S, LONDON ■ (OPPOSITE BOTTOM) FRONT COVER SHOWS A SECTION OF "ANGEL PLAYING THE LUTE" BY ROSSO FIORENTINO (1494–1540) FROM GALLERIA DEGLI UFFIZI, FLORENCE PERFORMING ARTISTS: VARIOUS ALBUM TITLES: VARIOUS

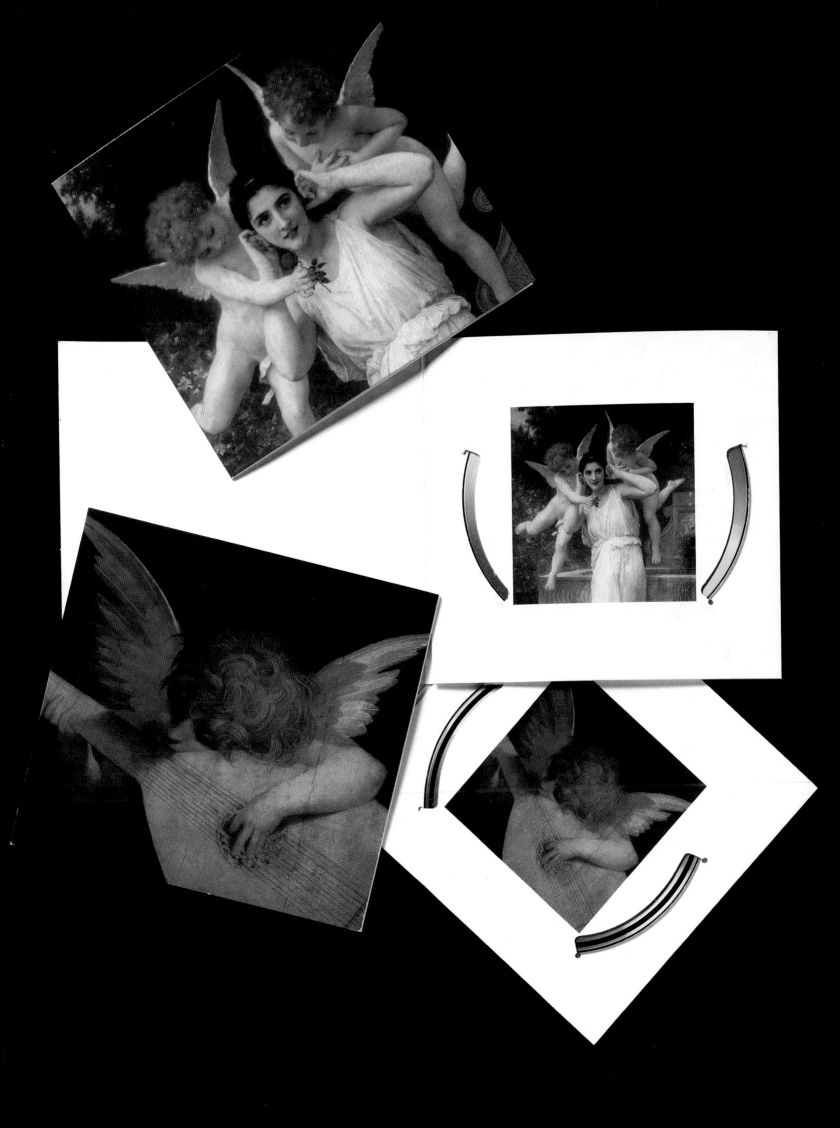

(OPPOSITE PAGE TOP LEFT) RECORD COMPANY: COLUMBIA RECORDS ART DIRECTOR: ARNOLD LEVINE PHOTOGRAPHER: JOSEF ASTOR
PERFORMING ARTIST: HARRY CONNICK, JR. ALBUM TITLE: WE ARE IN LOVE ■ (OPPOSITE TOP RIGHT) RECORD COMPANY: CAPITOL RECORDS
ART DIRECTOR: TOMMY STEELE DESIGNER/ILLUSTRATOR: ANDY ENGEL PHOTOGRAPHER: CAPITOL ARCHIVE PERFORMING ARTIST: NAT KING

COLE ALBUM TITLE: COLLECTORS SERIES ■ (OPPOSITE PAGE CENTER LEFT TO BOTTOM RIGHT) RECORD COMPANY: SONY MUSIC ART
DIRECTOR: ALLEN WEINBERG DESIGNER: ALLEN WEINBERG PERFORMING ARTIST: JOHNNY MATHIS ALBUM TITLE: THE MUSIC OF JOHNNY
MATHIS ■ (ABOVE) RECORD COMPANY: COLUMBIA/LEGACY ART DIRECTOR/DESIGNER: MARK BURDETT PHOTOGRAPHER: GREGORY HEISLER
TYPE DESIGN: LOUISE FILI PERFORMING ARTIST: TONY BENNETT ALBUM TITLE: FORTY YEARS: THE ARTISTRY OF TONY BENNETT, VOL. 4

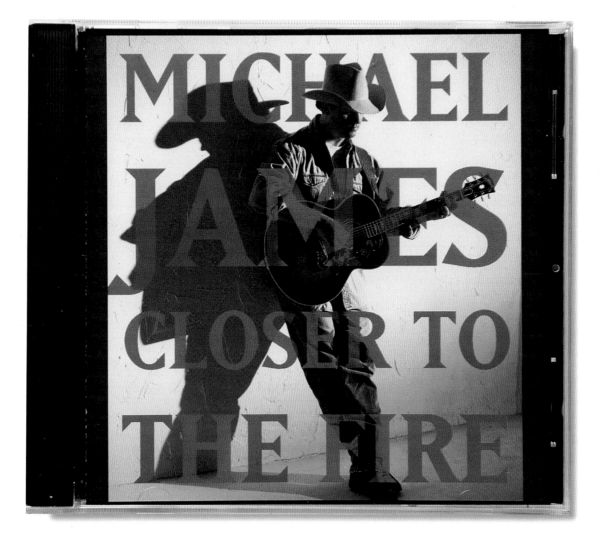

(THIS PAGE) RECORD COMPANY: REUNION RECORDS ART DIRECTORS: BUDDY JACKSON, D. RHODES DESIGNERS: SAM KNIGHT, JACKSON DESIGN PHOTOGRAPHER: MARK TUCKER DESIGN FIRM: JACKSON DESIGN PERFORMING ARTIST: MICHAEL JAMES ALBUM TITLE:

CLOSER TO THE FIRE ■ (THIS PAGE) RECORD COMPANY: HOLLYWOOD RECORDS ART DIRECTORS: JOE ELY, TERRY ALLEN ILLUS-
TRATORS: JOE ELY, TERRY ALLEN DESIGNER: MARIA DeGRASSI PERFORMING ARTISTS: VARIOUS ALBUM TITLE: SONGS FROM CHIPPY

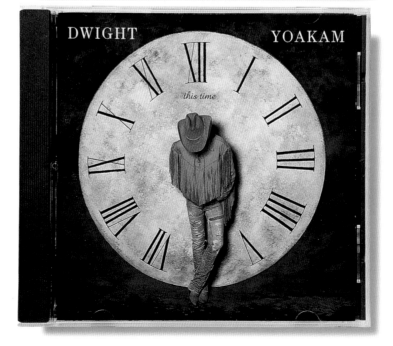

(THIS SPREAD)
RECORD COMPANY: SUB POP ART DIRECTOR/DESIGNER: ART CHANTRY
PERFORMING ARTIST: THE REVEREND HORTON HEAT
ALBUM TITLE: THE FULL-CUSTOM SOUNDS OF THE REVEREND HORTON HEAT

(OPPOSITE TOP) RECORD COMPANY: ATLANTIC RECORDS ART DIRECTOR: LARRY FREEMANTLE PHOTOGRAPHER: AMY GUIP PERFORMING ARTIST: DAS EFX ALBUM TITLE: STRAIGHT UP SEWASIDE ■ (OPPOSITE CENTER) RECORD COMPANY: RAP NATION RECORDS ART DIRECTOR/DESIGNER/ ILLUSTRATOR: WOLFGANG VON GERAMB DESIGN FIRM: HEADCHARGE PERFORMING ARTIST: STATE OF DEPARTMENTZ ALBUM TITLE: REIMEXPLOSION

■ (OPPOSITE BOTTOM) RECORD COMPANY: ATLANTIC RECORDS ART DIRECTOR: LYNN KOWALEWSKI PHOTOGRAPHER: MERLYN ROSENBERG PERFORM- ING ARTIST: MC LYTE ALBUM TITLE: AIN'T NO OTHER ■ (THIS PAGE) RECORD COMPANY: TOMMY BOY MUSIC ART DIRECTOR: ERWIN GOROSTIZA DESIGNERS: ART INDUSTRIA, ERIC SPILLMAN PHOTOGRAPHER: MICHAEL MILLER PERFORMING ARTIST: COOLIO ALBUM TITLE: IT TAKES A THIEF

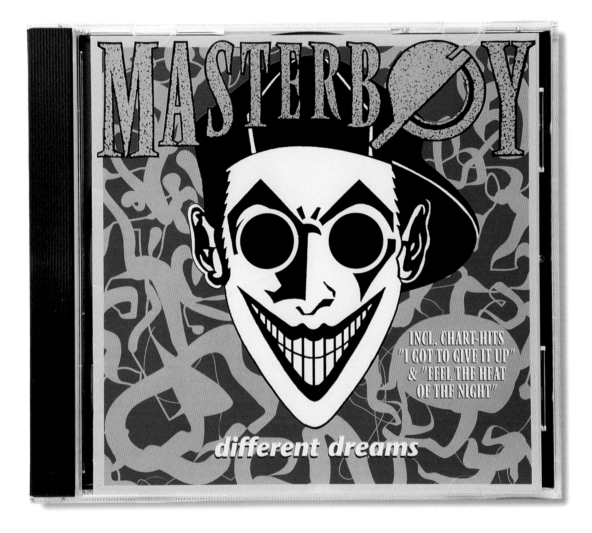

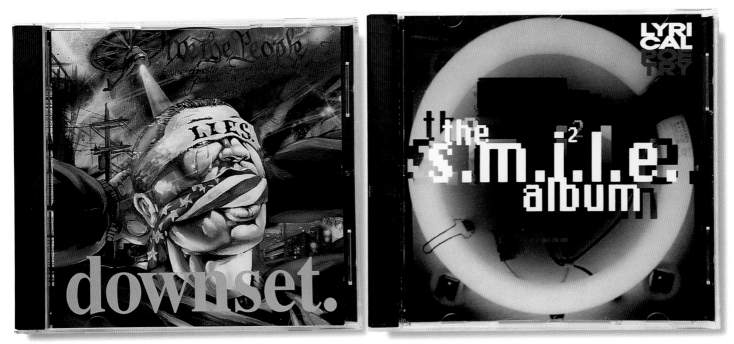

(OPPOSITE PAGE) RECORD COMPANY: POLYGRAM RECORDS ART DIRECTOR: MANFRED BAER DESIGNER: GOUTTE GRAFIK DESIGN PHOTOGRAPHER: FIN COSTELLO PERFORMING ARTIST: MASTERBOY ALBUM TITLE: DIFFERENT DREAMS ■ (THIS PAGE TOP LEFT) RECORD COMPANY: POLYGRAM RECORDS ART DIRECTOR: BARRY GREENHUT DESIGNERS: DOWNSET, BARRY GREENHUT ILLUSTRATOR: MEAR PERFORMING ARTIST/ALBUM TITLE: DOWNSET ■ (THIS PAGE TOP RIGHT) RECORD COMPANY: SUB UP RECORDS DESIGNERS: STEFAN RUECKERL, ANDREAS DOEHRING PHOTOGRAPHER: PETER KEMPTER DESIGN FIRM: RUECKERL/DOEHRING PERFORMING ARTIST: LYRICAL POETRY ALBUM TITLE: THE S.M.I².L.E. ALBUM ■ (THIS PAGE BOTTOM LEFT) RECORD COMPANY: COLUMBIA RECORDS ART DIRECTOR: STACY DRUMMOND DESIGNER: STACY DRUMMOND ASSISTANT DESIGNER: JULIAN PEPLOE PHOTOGRAPHER: MICHAEL MILLER DESIGN FIRM: SONY MUSIC PERFORMING ARTIST: KRIS KROSS ALBUM TITLE: DA BOMB ■ (THIS PAGE BOTTOM RIGHT) RECORD COMPANY: RUFF HOUSE/COLUMBIA ART DIRECTOR: SARA ROTMAN DESIGNER: DANA SHIMIZU ILLUSTRATOR: VINNIE ANGEL PERFORMING ARTIST: GOATS ALBUM TITLE: TRICKS OF THE SHADE

(THIS SPREAD)

RECORD COMPANY: MCA RECORDS ART DIRECTOR: VARTAN

DESIGNER/MODEL DESIGN: RON LARSON PERFORMING ARTISTS: VARIOUS

ALBUM TITLE: THE FLINTSTONES

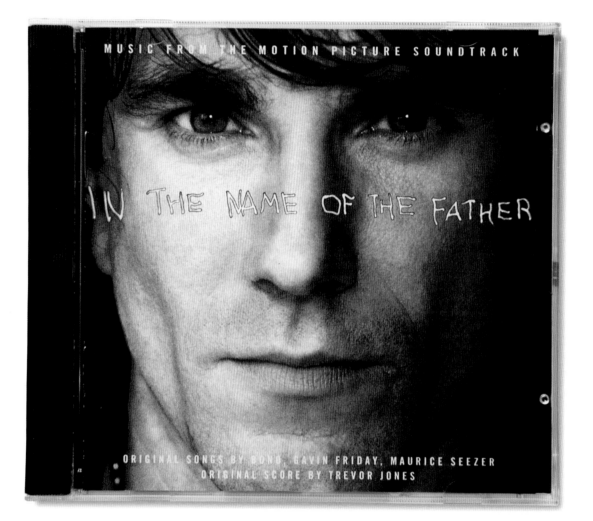

(THIS PAGE) RECORD COMPANY: ISLAND RECORDS ART DIRECTOR/DESIGNER: CALLY PHOTOGRAPHER: JONATHAN HESSION (PHOTOGRAPH AND TITLE © UNIVERSAL CITY STUDIOS, INC.) DESIGN FIRM: ART ISLAND PERFORMING ARTISTS: VARIOUS ALBUM TITLE: IN THE NAME OF THE FATHER ■ (OPPOSITE PAGE) RECORD COMPANY: EPIC SOUNDTRACKS DESIGNER: ENDRE KORANYI PHOTO: CASTLE ROCK ENTERTAINMENT DESIGN FIRM: SONY MUSIC CREATIVE SERVICES PERFORMING ARTIST: VARIOUS ALBUM TITLE: THE SHAWSHANK REDEMPTION

(OPPOSITE TOP LEFT) RECORD COMPANY: © 1990 WARNER BROS. RECORDS/WEA INTERNATIONAL INC. ART DIRECTOR/DESIGNER: TOM RECCHION ILLUSTRATOR/PHOTOGRAPHER: WARNER BROS. ANIMATION ARCHIVES DESIGN FIRM: WARNER BROS. IN-HOUSE ART DEPT PERFORMING ARTIST: CARL STALLING PROJECT ALBUM TITLE: MUSIC FROM WARNER BROS. CARTOONS 1936–1958 ■ (TOP RIGHT) RECORD COMPANY: VERVE RECORDS ART DIRECTOR/ DESIGNER: DAVID LAU DESIGN FIRM: IN-HOUSE PERFORMING ARTIST: FRED ASTAIRE ALBUM TITLE: STEPPIN' OUT: ASTAIRE SINGS ■ (MIDDLE LEFT) RECORD COMPANY: INTERCORD TON GMBH ART DIRECTORS: SUSANNE WACKER, WOLFRAM SCHÄFFER DESIGNER/ ILLUSTRATOR: STEFAN SCHMID DESIGN FIRM: DESIGN HOCH DREI PERFORMING ARTIST: DA' CHOICE ALBUM TITLE: MAKE THAT MOVE ■ (MIDDLE

RIGHT) RECORD COMPANY: POINT MUSIC/POLYGRAM RECORDS ART DIRECTOR: MARGERY GREENSPAN DESIGNER: DAVID LAU DESIGN FIRM: IN-HOUSE PERFORMING ARTIST: GAVIN BRYARS ALBUM TITLE: THE SINKING OF THE TITANIC ■ (BOTTOM LEFT) RECORD COMPANY: REC REC MUSIC ART DIRECTOR: PETER BÄDER PHOTOGRAPHER: OSCAR SALGADO PERFORMING ARTIST: FRED FRITA ALBUM TITLE: STEP ACROSS THE BORDER ■ (BOTTOM RIGHT) RECORD COMPANY: POLYGRAM RECORDS ART DIRECTOR/DESIGNER: DAVID LAU DESIGN FIRM: IN-HOUSE PERFORMING ARTISTS: VARIOUS ALBUM TITLE: MI VIDA LOCA ■ (ABOVE) RECORD COMPANY: BMG ARIOLA ART DIRECTOR/DESIGNER: VERONICA KUMLIN D'OREY IMAGE MANIPULATION: VERONICA KUMLIN D'OREY PHOTOGRAPHER: LEVINDO CARNEIRO PERFORMING ARTIST: VARIOUS ALBUM TITLE: DANCE TECHNO DANCE 2

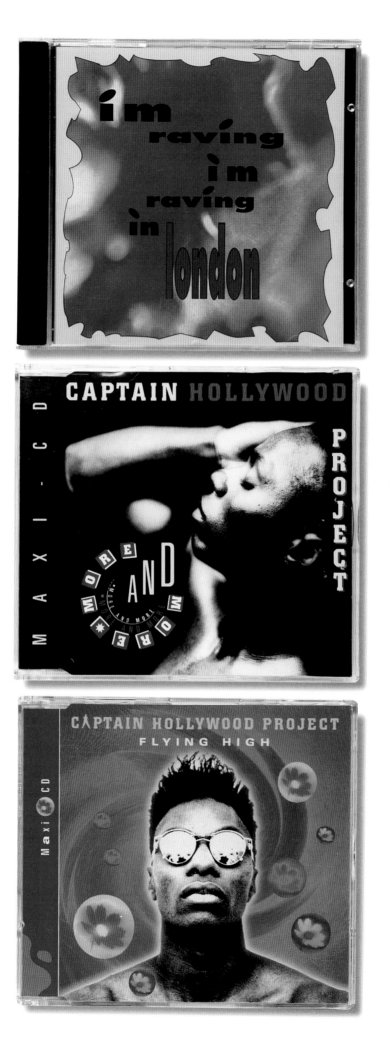

(OPPOSITE LEFT AND ABOVE) RECORD COMPANY: MBC RECORDS ART DIRECTOR/DESIGNER: MARIANNE VON ALLESCH DESIGN FIRM: SPV GRAPHICS PERFORMING ARTISTS: VARIOUS ALBUM TITLE: I'M RAVING I'M RAVING IN LONDON ■ (OPPOSITE CENTER) RECORD COMPANY: INTERCORD TON GMBH ART DIRECTORS/DESIGNERS: SUSANNE WACKER, WOLFRAM SCHÄFFER PHOTOGRAPHERS: ESSER & STRAUSS DESIGN FIRM: DESIGN HOCH DREI PERFORMING ARTIST: CAPTAIN HOLLYWOOD PROJECT ALBUM TITLE: MORE AND MORE REMIXES ■ (OPPOSITE BOTTOM AND THIS PAGE BOTTOM) RECORD COMPANY: INTERCORD TON GMBH ART DIRECTORS/DESIGNERS: SUSANNE WACKER, WOLFRAM SCHÄFFER PHOTOGRAPHER: HELGE STRAUSS DESIGN FIRM: DESIGN HOCH DREI PERFORMING ARTIST: CAPTAIN HOLLYWOOD PROJECT ALBUM TITLE: FLYING HIGH

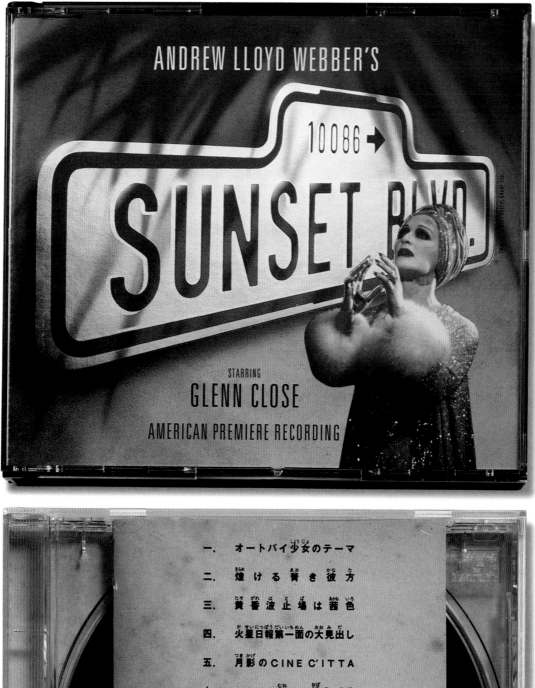

(OPPOSITE PAGE TOP AND THIS PAGE TOP) RECORD COMPANY: REALLY USEFUL RECORDS DESIGNER: SERINO COYNE, INC. PHOTOGRAPHER: JOAN MARCUS PERFORMING ARTISTS: VARIOUS ALBUM TITLE: SUNSET BOULEVARD ■ (OPPOSITE PAGE BOTTOM AND THIS PAGE BOTTOM) RECORD COMPANY: KITTY ENTERPRISES, INC. ART DIRECTOR/DESIGNER: YOSHIRO NAKAMURA DESIGN FIRM: YEN INC.

(THIS PAGE) RECORD COMPANY: SIX 6 RECORDS DESIGNER: NICK GUNDILL PERFORMING ARTISTS: RENAISSANCE WITH SASHA & JOHN DIGWEED ALBUM TITLE: RENAISSANCE, THE MIX COLLECTION ■ (OPPOSITE PAGE) RECORD COMPANY: EMIGRE RECORDS ART DIRECTOR: RUDY VANDERLANS DESIGNER: RUDY VANDERLANS PERFORMING ARTIST: BASEHEAD ALBUM TITLE: PLAY WITH TOYS

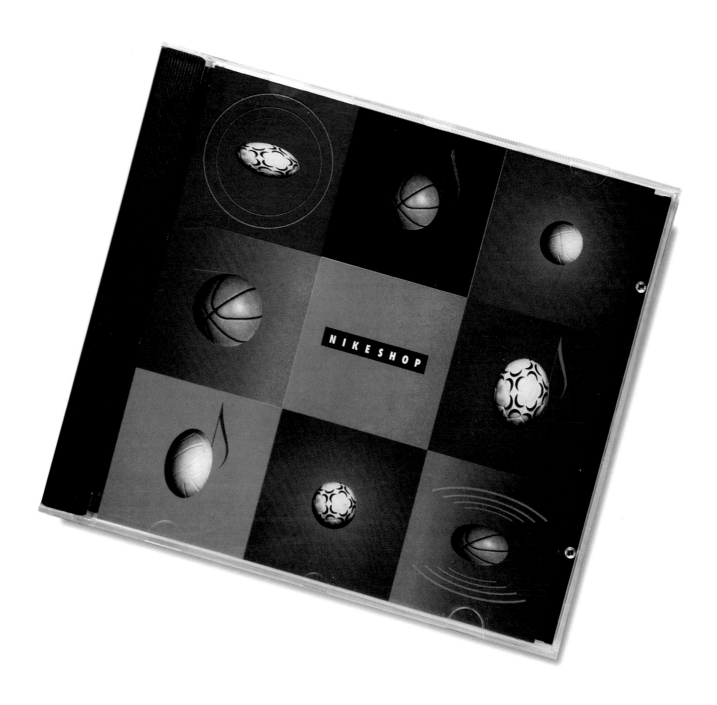

(OPPOSITE) ART DIRECTOR/DESIGNER: MICHELE MELANDRI DESIGN FIRM: NIKE DESIGN PERFORMING ARTISTS: NORMAN DURKEE, ROB WHITESIDES WOO, CASEY JAMES ALBUM TITLE: NIKE SHOP ■ (ABOVE) RECORD COMPANY: © 1991 WARNER BROS./OPAL RECORDS ART DIRECTOR/DESIGNER: TOM RECCHION PHOTOGRAPHER: HAROLD BUDD DESIGN FIRM: WARNER BROS. IN-HOUSE ART DEPT PERFORMING ARTIST: HAROLD BUDD ALBUM TITLE: BY THE DAWN'S EARLY LIGHT ■ (BELOW) RECORD COMPANY: STRANGE WAYS RECORDS ART DIRECTOR: PETER W. CZERNICH ILLUSTRATOR: EVA METHFESSEL DESIGN FIRM: TECHCOM GMBH PERFORMING ARTIST: PERON BERKOVITZ ALBUM TITLE: TERMINATRIX

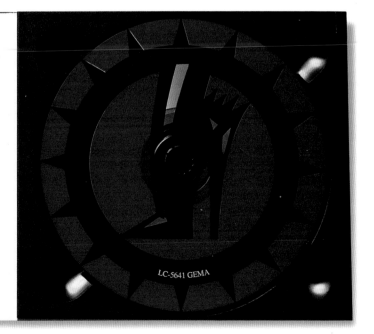

(OPPOSITE) RECORD COMPANY: ANGEL RECORDS ART DIRECTOR: JAY BARBIERI ILLUSTRATOR: MARVIN MATTELSON PERFORMING ARTIST: THE BENEDICTINE MONKS OF SANTO DOMINGO DE SILOS ALBUM TITLE: CHANT ■ (BELOW TOP) RECORD COMPANY: © 1992 WARNER BROS. RECORDS ART DIRECTOR: JERI HEIDEN DESIGNER: GREG ROSS PHOTOGRAPHERS: ANN CUTTING, ELISABETH FERYN DESIGN FIRM: WARNER

BROS. IN-HOUSE ART DEPT PERFORMING ARTIST: LOREENA MCKENNITT ALBUM TITLE: THE VISIT ■ (ABOVE CENTER) RECORD COMPANY: ESTRUS RECORDS ART DIRECTOR: ART CHANTRY DESIGNER: ART CHANTRY PERFORMING ARTIST: THE MONO MEN ALBUM TITLE: WRECKER! ■ (ABOVE BOTTOM) RECORD COMPANY: ESTRUS RECORDS ART DIRECTOR/DESIGNER: ART CHANTRY ALBUM TITLE: DESTROY ALL ASTROMEN!

(OPPOSITE TOP) RECORD COMPANY: EMIGRE RECORDS ART DIRECTOR: RUDY VANDERLANS PHOTOGRAPHER: JOSEPH RICHARD NEGRO
PERFORMING ARTIST: SUPERCOLLIDER ALBUM TITLE: DUAL ■ (OPPOSITE CENTER) RECORD COMPANY: EMIGRE RECORDS ART DIRECTOR/DESIGNER:
RUDY VANDERLANS ILLUSTRATOR: EDWARD FELLA PERFORMING ARTIST: HONEY BARBARA ALBUM TITLE: FEEDLOTLOOPHOLE ■ (OPPOSITE BOT-

TOM) RECORD COMPANY: EMIGRE RECORDS ART DIRECTOR/DESIGNER: RUDY VANDERLANS PHOTOGRAPHER: DAN OLSEN PERFORMING ARTISTS:
VARIOUS ALBUM TITLE: EMIGRE MUSIC SAMPLER #2 ■ (ABOVE) RECORD COMPANY: POLYDOR RECORDS ART DIRECTOR: ANDY GREETHAM
DESIGNERS: ANDY GREETHAM, KELLY DUNN PERFORMING ARTIST: JEAN MICHEL JARRE ALBUM TITLE: SLAM & GAT DECOR REMIXES

(THIS PAGE AND OPPOSITE CENTER) RECORD COMPANY: RECYCLE OR DIE/EYE Q MUSIC ART DIRECTOR/DESIGNER: LOUIS A. FLANIGAN, JR. COVER PAINTING: ROBERT LONGO: "TRIB" DESIGN FIRM: ARE U READY? PERFORMING ARTIST: DOMINIC WOOSEY ALBUM TITLE: STRAYLIGHT ■ (OPPOSITE TOP) RECORD COMPANY: STRANGE WAYS ART DIRECTOR: BRÜCKE 5, HAMBURG DESIGNER: BRÜCKE 5, HAMBURG ILLUSTRATOR:

ZINCOGRAPHIC COPY BASED ON A PICTURE BY GUSTAVE DORÉ DESIGN FIRM: BRÜCKE 5, HAMBURG PERFORMING ARTIST: CARLOS PERON ALBUM TITLE: DIE SCHÖPFUNG DER WELT ODER SIEBEN TAGE GOTTES ■ (OPPOSITE BOTTOM) RECORD COMPANY: WARNER BROS. RECORDS/© QUINLAN ROAD LTD. ART DIRECTOR: JEFF GOLD DESIGNER: LOREENA MCKINNITT ILLUSTRATOR: MARGO CHASE PHOTOGRAPHER: ANN ELLIOT-CUTTING DESIGN FIRM: MARGO CHASE DESIGN ARTIST: LOREENA MCKINNITT ALBUM TITLE: THE MASK AND MIRROR

(TOP ROW) RECORD COMPANY: MARLBORO MUSIC ART DIRECTOR: HANS HAMMERS, JR. II DESIGNER: WOLFGANG VON GERAMB ILLUSTRATOR: MICHAEL MAU DESIGN FIRM: HEADCHARGE W.A. PERFORMING ARTIST: LONDON UNDERGROUND ALBUM TITLE: VOLUME 3 ■ (BOTTOM ROW) RECORD COMPANY: ATLANTIC RECORDS DESIGNER: GREENBERG KINGSLEY PERFORMING ARTIST: GINGER BAKER TRIO ALBUM TITLE: GOING BACK HOME

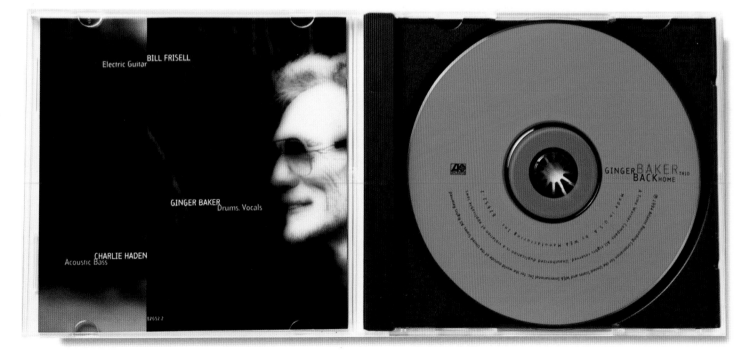

OPPOSITE PAGE) RECORD COMPANY: SONY MUSIC ART DIRECTOR: MARK BURDETT DESIGNERS: SPARK/JULIAN PAPLOV PHOTOGRAPHERS: VARIOUS PERFORMING ARTISTS: VARIOUS ALBUM TITLE: VARIOUS ■ (THIS PAGE) RECORD COMPANY: SONY MUSIC ART DIRECTOR/DESIGNER: ALLEN WEINBERG PHOTOGRAPHERS: VARIOUS DESIGN FIRM: SONY MUSIC PERFORMING ARTISTS: VARIOUS ALBUM TITLE: THE ESSENCE OF...

(OPPOSITE) Record Company: IMPROMUSIC Art Director: MARKUS HUBER Designer: MARKUS HUBER Performing Artist: IMPROVISESSION Album Title: AN ACOUSTIC EVENING ■ (ABOVE) Record Company: GRP RECORDS Creative Director: ANDY BALTIMORE Designer: SCOTT JOHNSON Photographer: CHARLES STEWART Performing Artist: IMPULSE! Album Title: A 30 YEAR CELEBRATION

(THIS PAGE) RECORD COMPANY: VIDEOARTS MUSIC, INC. ART DIRECTOR/DESIGNER: KEISUKE UNOSAWA DESIGN FIRM: KEISUKE UNOSAWA DESIGN PERFORMING ARTIST: YOSHIO "CHIN" SUZUKI ALBUM TITLE: THE MOMENT ■ (OPPOSITE PAGE TOP) RECORD COMPANY: GRP RECORDS CREATIVE DIRECTOR: ANDY BALTIMORE ART DIRECTOR: SONNY MEDIANA DESIGNER: ALBA ACEVEDO PHOTOGRAPHER: EJ CAMP PERFORMING ARTIST: ROB WASSERMAN ALBUM TITLE: TRIOS ■ (OPPOSITE PAGE CENTER) RECORD COMPANY: GRP RECORDS CREATIVE

DIRECTOR: ANDY BALTIMORE ART DIRECTOR: SCOTT JOHNSON DESIGNERS: ALBA ACEVEDO, JACKIE SALWAY ILLUSTRATOR: SCOTT JOHNSON PHOTOGRAPHER: SAM URDANK PERFORMING ARTISTS: PHIL WOODS & RAY BROWN ALBUM TITLE: AMERICAN JAZZ PHILHARMONIC ■ (OPPO-SITE PAGE BOTTOM) RECORD COMPANY: GRP RECORDS ART DIRECTOR: SONNY MEDIANA DESIGNERS: LAURIE GOLDMAN, ALBA ACEVEDO ILLUSTRATOR: JOEL NAKAMURA PHOTOGRAPHER: PEGGY PIKE PERFORMING ARTIST: DON GRUSIN ALBUM TITLE: BANANA FISH

RECORD COMPANY: COLUMBIA JAZZ/SONY MUSIC
ART DIRECTOR: TRACY BOYCHUK
PHOTOGRAPHER: ANDREW ECCLES
DESIGN FIRM: SONY MUSIC CREATIVE SERVICES
PERFORMING ARTIST: DAVID SANCHEZ
ALBUM TITLE: THE DEPARTURES

RECORD COMPANY: © 1993 WARNER BROS. RECORDS/WEA INTERNATIONAL INC.

ART DIRECTORS: JEFF GOLD, JERI HEIDEN

DESIGNER: JOHN HEIDEN

PHOTOGRAPHER: ANNIE LEIBOVITZ

DESIGN FIRM: WARNER BROS. IN-HOUSE ART DEPARTMENT

PERFORMING ARTISTS: MILES DAVIS, QUINCY JONES

ALBUM TITLE: MILES & QUINCY: LIVE AT MONTREUX

(OPPOSITE TOP LEFT) RECORD COMPANY: GRP RECORDS CREATIVE DIRECTOR: ANDY BALTIMORE ART DIRECTOR/ILLUSTRATOR: DAN SERRANO DESIGNER: ALBA ACEVEDO PHOTOGRAPHER: CARL STUDNA PERFORMING ARTIST: THE BENOIT FREEMAN PROJECT ALBUM TITLE: THE BENOIT FREEMAN PROJECT ■ (TOP RIGHT) RECORD COMPANY: GRP RECORDS CREATIVE DIRECTOR: ANDY BALTIMORE ART DIRECTOR: DAN SERRANO DESIGNERS: ALBA ACEVEDO, JACKIE SALWAY ILLUSTRATOR: RALPH PRATA PHOTOGRAPHER: DARRYL PITT PERFORMING ARTIST: JOHN PATITUCCI ALBUM TITLE: ANOTHER WORLD ■ (CENTER LEFT) RECORD COMPANY: GRP RECORDS CREATIVE DIRECTOR: ANDY BALTIMORE ILLUSTRATOR: JOHN BRAINARD PHOTOGRAPHER: PHIL ONOFRIO PERFORMING ARTIST: RAMSEY LEWIS ALBUM TITLE: SKY ISLANDS ■ (CENTER RIGHT) RECORD COMPANY: GRP RECORDS CREATIVE DIRECTOR: ANDY BALTIMORE ILLUSTRATOR: PAUL PASCARELLA PERFORMING ARTISTS: DAVE GRUSIN, DON

GRUSIN ALBUM TITLE: STICKS & BONES ■ (OPPOSITE BOTTOM LEFT) RECORD COMPANY: GRP RECORDS CREATIVE DIRECTOR: ANDY BALTIMORE ART DIRECTOR: DAN SERRANO DESIGNERS: ALBA ACEVEDO, FREDDIE PALOMA, LAURIE GOLDMAN ILLUSTRATOR: TOR LUNDVALL PHOTOGRAPHER: CAROL WEINBERG PERFORMING ARTIST: BOB BERG ALBUM TITLE: RIDDLES ■ (BOTTOM RIGHT) RECORD COMPANY: GRP RECORDS CREATIVE DIRECTOR: ANDY BALTIMORE ART DIRECTOR: HOLLIS KING DESIGNER: FREDDIE PALOMA ILLUSTRATOR: HOLLIS KING PERFORMING ARTIST: BROWNSTONES AND MOONLIGHT ALBUM TITLE: A CELEBRATION OF BLACK MUSIC MONTH ■ (ABOVE) RECORD COMPANY: GRP RECORDS CREATIVE DIRECTOR: ANDY BALTIMORE ART DIRECTOR: MICHAEL MANOOGIAN DESIGNERS: DAN SERRANO, DAVID GIBB, ANDY RUGGIRELLO, SCOTT JOHNSON, SONNY MEDIANA PHOTOGRAPHER: HANS NELEMAN PERFORMING ARTIST: JOHN PATITUCCI ALBUM TITLE: HEART OF THE BASS

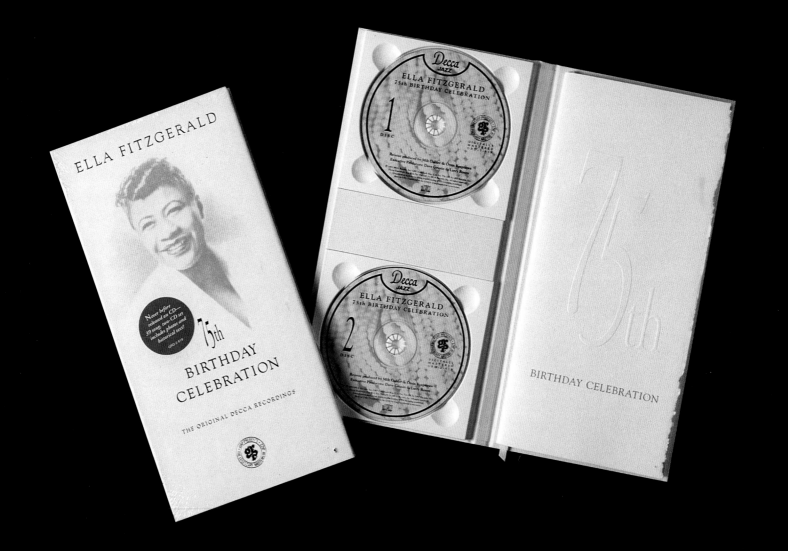

(OPPOSITE PAGE) RECORD COMPANY: SONY MUSIC ART DIRECTOR: MARK BURDETT DESIGNER: MARK BURDETT PHOTOGRAPHERS: VARIOUS
PERFORMING ARTISTS: VARIOUS ALBUM TITLE: SWING TIME 1-3 ■ (THIS PAGE) RECORD COMPANY: GRP RECORDS CREATIVE DIRECTOR: ANDY
BALTIMORE ART DIRECTOR: SCOTT JOHNSON PERFORMING ARTIST: ELLA FITZGERALD ALBUM TITLE: 75TH BIRTHDAY CELEBRATION

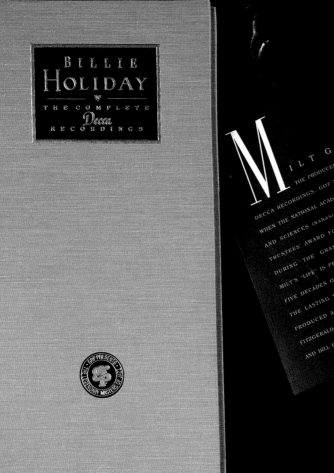

MILT GABLER

THE PRODUCER OF BILLIE HOLIDAY'S DECCA RECORDINGS, GOT HIS JUST DUE IN 1991 WHEN THE NATIONAL ACADEMY OF RECORDING ARTS AND SCIENCES (NARAS) PRESENTED HIM WITH A TRUSTEES' AWARD FOR LIFETIME ACHIEVEMENT DURING THE GRAMMY AWARDS CEREMONIES. MILT'S LIFE IS PERMANENTLY INTERTWINED WITH FIVE DECADES OF JAZZ AND POPULAR MUSIC AND THE LASTING VALUE OF THE ARTISTS WORK HE PRODUCED AND PROMOTED. FROM BILLIE, ELLA FITZGERALD, AND BING CROSBY TO LOUIS JORDAN AND BILL HALEY, IS INDISPUTABLE AND INDELIBLE.

ARTHUR HERZOG, JR.
AND BILLIE HOLIDAY

(OPPOSITE AND ABOVE RIGHT) RECORD COMPANY: MCA RECORDS ART DIRECTOR: VARTAN DESIGNER: ANDY ENGEL PERFORMING ARTIST: BILLIE HOLIDAY
ALBUM TITLE: THE COMPLETE DECCA RECORDINGS ■ (ABOVE LEFT) RECORD COMPANY: SONY MUSIC ART DIRECTOR/DESIGNER: ALLEN WEINBERG PHOTOG-
RAPHER: BILL GOTTLIEB BOOKLET INTERIOR: BILL GOTTLIEB AND UNKNOWN PERFORMING ARTIST: BILLIE HOLIDAY ALBUM TITLE: THE LEGACY BOX SET

Ryan Kisor
On the One

Alex Bugnon This Time Around

Les McCann
ON THE SOUL SIDE

LONDON UNDERGROUND
THE REAL GROOVE OF THE NINETIES
VOLUME II
A NIGHT ON THE TOWN

OLETA ADAMS EVOLUTION

Grover Washington, Jr.
All My Tomorrows

(OPPOSITE TOP LEFT) RECORD COMPANY: SONY MUSIC ART DIRECTOR/DESIGNER: MARK BURDETT PHOTOGRAPHER: FRANK W. OCKENFELS III PERFORMING ARTIST: RYAN KISOR ALBUM TITLE: ON THE ONE ■ (TOP RIGHT) RECORD COMPANY: SONY MUSIC ART DIRECTOR/DESIGNER: ALLEN WEINBERG PHOTOGRAPHER: MARC HAUSER PERFORMING ARTIST: ALEX BUGNON ALBUM TITLE: THIS TIME AROUND ■ (OPPOSITE CENTER LEFT) RECORD COMPANY: COLUMBIA RECORDS ART DIRECTOR/DESIGNER: JIM DEBARROS PHOTOGRAPHER: ANDREW ECCLES PERFORMING ARTIST: LES MCCANN ALBUM TITLE: ON THE SOUL SIDE ■ (CENTER RIGHT AND THIS PAGE) RECORD COMPANY: MARLBORO MUSIC/HEADCHARGE ART

DIRECTOR: HANS HAMMERS, JR. II DESIGNER: WOLFGANG VON GERAMB PHOTOGRAPHY: IMAGEBANK DESIGN FIRM: HEADCHARGE PERFORMING ARTIST: LONDON UNDERGROUND ALBUM TITLE: VOLUME 2: A NIGHT ON THE TOWN ■ (OPPOSITE BOTTOM LEFT) RECORD COMPANY: POLYGRAM RECORDS DESIGNERS: ANDREW BISCOMB, PETER BARRETT PHOTOGRAPHER: RANDEE ST. NICOLAS PERFORMING ARTIST: OLETA ADAMS ALBUM TITLE: EVOLUTION ■ (OPPOSITE BOTTOM RIGHT) RECORD COMPANY: SONY MUSIC ART DIRECTOR: ALLEN WEINBERG DESIGNER: ALLEN WEINBERG PHOTOGRAPHER: NANA WATANABE PERFORMING ARTIST: GROVER WASHINGTON, JR. ALBUM TITLE: ALL MY TOMORROWS

RECORD COMPANY: SONY MUSIC

ART DIRECTOR/DESIGNER: ALLEN WEINBERG

PHOTOGRAPHER: BRAD GUICE

PERFORMING ARTIST/ALBUM TITLE: DWIGHT SILLS

RECORD COMPANY: SONY MUSIC

ART DIRECTOR/DESIGNER: ALLEN WEINBERG

PERFORMING ARTIST: ROSKO

ALBUM TITLE: PRIVATE MOMENTS

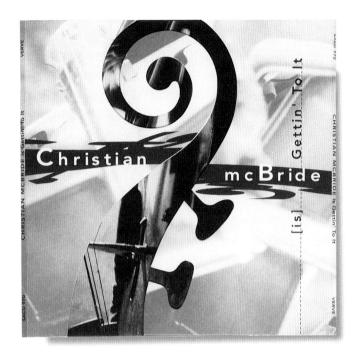

(OPPOSITE TOP) RECORD COMPANY: VERVE RECORDS/POLYGRAM RECORDS ART DIRECTOR/DESIGNER: LISA PO-YING HUANG ILLUSTRATOR: DAVID STONE MARTIN DESIGN FIRM: IN-HOUSE PERFORMING ARTISTS: VARIOUS ALBUM TITLE: THE JAZZ SCENE ■ (BOTTOM) RECORD COMPANY: VERVE RECORDS/POLYGRAM RECORDS ART DIRECTOR/DESIGNER: DAVID LAU DESIGN FIRM: IN-HOUSE PHOTOGRAPHER: JAMES MINCHIN PERFORMING ARTIST: ROY HARD GROVE ALBUM TITLE: WITH TENORS OF OUR TIME ■ (THIS PAGE) RECORD COMPANY: VERVE RECORDS/POLYGRAM RECORDS ART DIRECTOR: PATRICIA LIE PHOTOGRAPHER: JAMES MINCHIN PERFORMING ARTIST: CHRISTIAN MCBRIDE ALBUM TITLE: (IS) GETTIN' TO IT

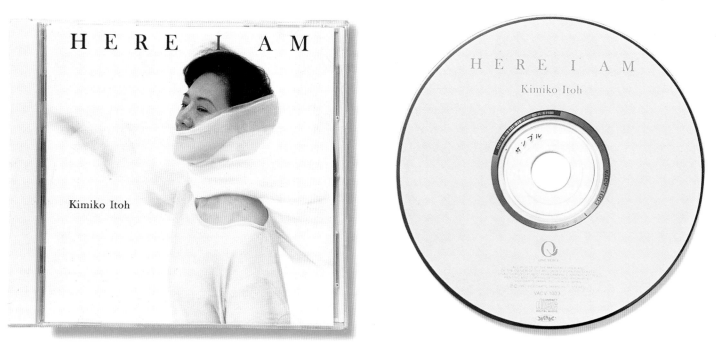

(THIS PAGE TOP) RECORD COMPANY: VIDEOARTS MUSIC, INC. ART DIRECTOR: KEISUKE UNOSAWA DESIGNER: KEISUKE UNOSAWA DESIGN FIRM: KEISUKE UNOSAWA DESIGN PERFORMING ARTIST: KIMIKO ITOH ALBUM TITLE: HERE I AM ■ (THIS PAGE BOTTOM) RECORD COMPANY: VIRGIN RECORDS ART DIRECTOR: JAMES O'MARA DESIGNER: JAMES O'MARA ILLUSTRATOR: JAMES O'MARA PHOTOGRAPHER: JAMES O'MARA DESIGN FIRM: O'MARA & RYAN PERFORMING ARTIST: COLIN JAMES AND THE LITTLE BIG BAND ALBUM TITLE: COLIN JAMES AND THE LITTLE BIG BAND ■ (OPPOSITE PAGE TOP LEFT) RECORD COMPANY: VIDEOARTS MUSIC, INC. ART DIRECTOR: KEISUKE UNOSAWA DESIGNER: KEISUKE UNOSAWA DESIGN FIRM: KEISUKE UNOSAWA DESIGN PERFORMING ARTIST: RYO KAWASAKI ALBUM TITLE:

HERE THERE AND EVERYWHERE ■ (THIS PAGE TOP RIGHT) RECORD COMPANY: SONY MUSIC ART DIRECTOR: ALLEN WEINBERG DESIGNER: ALLEN WEINBERG PHOTOGRAPHER: HERMAN LEONARD PERFORMING ARTIST: ERROLL GARNER ALBUM TITLE: SOLOS ■ (THIS PAGE BOTTOM LEFT) RECORD COMPANY: SONY MUSIC ART DIRECTOR: JIM DEBARROS DESIGNER: JIM DEBARROS PHOTOGRAPHER: ANDREW ECCLES PERFORMING ARTIST: TOSHIKO AKIYOSHI JAZZ ORCHESTRA ALBUM TITLE: DESERT LADY/FANTASY ■ (THIS PAGE BOTTOM RIGHT) RECORD COMPANY: © 1991 QWEST RECORDS ART DIRECTOR: JERI HEIDEN DESIGNER: LINDA COBB FRONT COVER PAINTING: JOEL NAKAMURA DESIGN FIRM: WARNER BROS. IN-HOUSE ART DEPT PERFORMING ARTIST: DORI CAYMMI ALBUM TITLE: BRASILIAN SERENATA

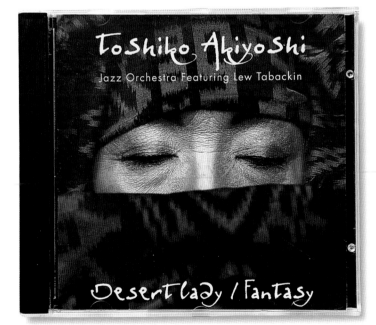

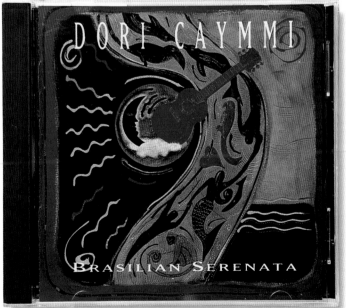

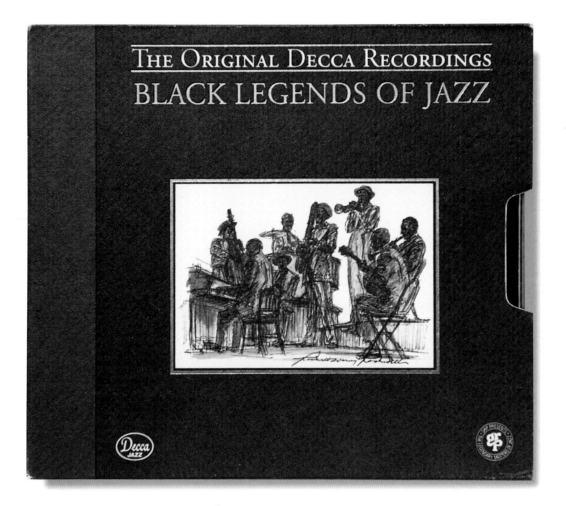

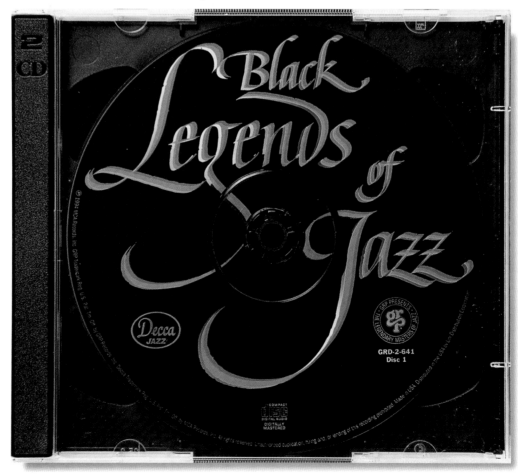

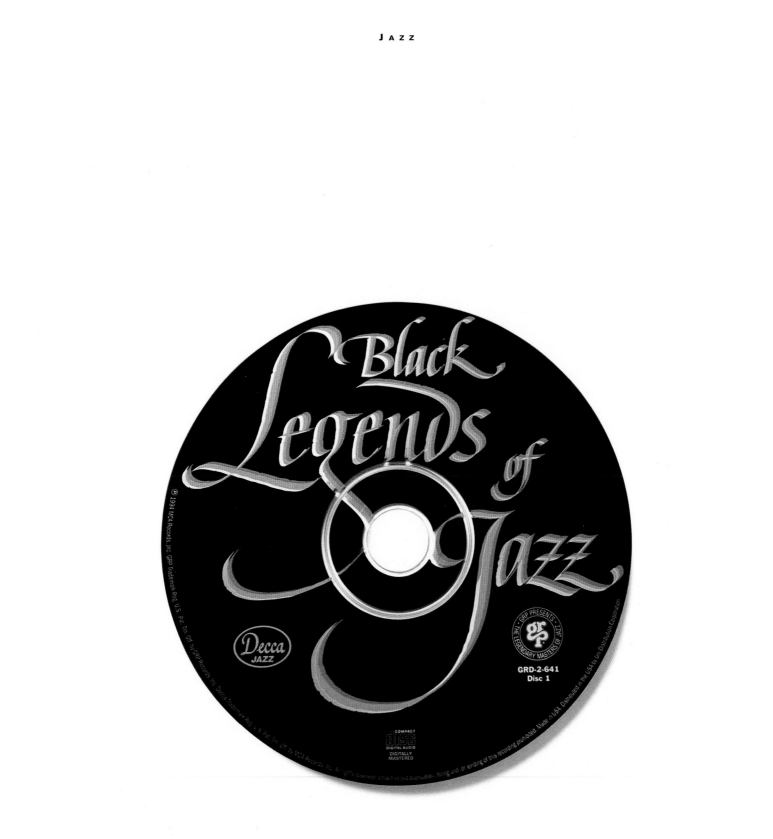

RECORD COMPANY: GRP RECORDS ART DIRECTORS: HOLLIS KING, DAN SERRANO DESIGNER: LAURIE GOLDMAN ILLUSTRATOR: RICHARD ROCKWELL PHOTOGRAPHERS: FROM THE FRANK DRIGGS COLLECTION, DUNCAN P. SCHIEDT ALBUM TITLE: BLACK LEGENDS OF JAZZ

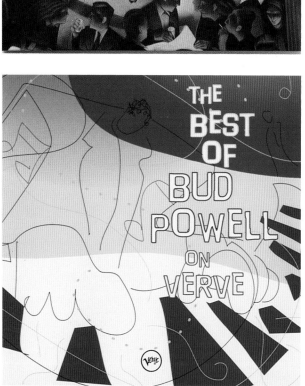

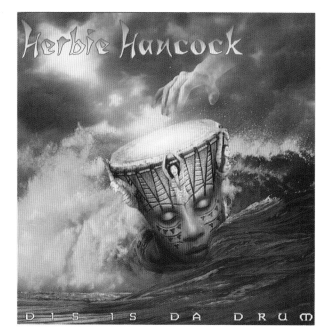

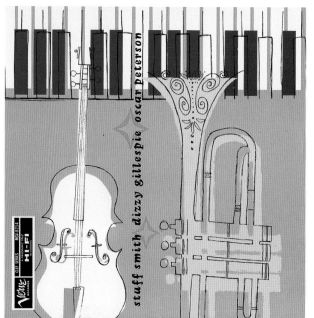

(OPPOSITE TOP LEFT) RECORD COMPANY: SONY MUSIC ART DIRECTOR/DESIGNER: ALLEN WEINBERG ILLUSTRATOR: GARY KELLY PERFORMING ARTISTS: VARIOUS ALBUM TITLE: THE JAZZ MASTERS ■ (OPPOSITE PAGE TOP RIGHT) RECORD COMPANY: VERVE RECORDS/POLYGRAM RECORDS ART DIRECTOR/DESIGNER: DAVID LAU PHOTOGRAPHER: JAMES MINCHIN DESIGN FIRM: IN-HOUSE PERFORMING ARTIST: ROY HARGROVE QUINTET ALBUM TITLE: WITH THE TENORS OF OUR TIME ■ (OPPOSITE PAGE CENTER LEFT) RECORD COMPANY: VERVE RECORDS/ POLYGRAM RECORDS ART DIRECTOR: DAVID LAU DESIGNERS: LISA PO-YING HUANG, DAVID LAU ILLUSTRATOR: CHUNG DEH-TIEN DESIGN FIRM: IN-HOUSE PERFORMING ARTIST: BUD POWELL ALBUM TITLE: THE BEST OF BUD POWELL ON VERVE ■ (OPPOSITE PAGE, CENTER RIGHT) RECORD COMPANY: VERVE RECORDS/POLYGRAM RECORDS ART DIRECTOR/DESIGNER: LISA PO-YING HUANG ILLUSTRATOR: DAVID

STONE MARTIN PERFORMING ARTIST: ILLINOIS JACQUET ALBUM TITLE: FLYING HOME: THE BEST OF THE VERVE YEARS ■ (OPPOSITE PAGE, BOTTOM LEFT) RECORD COMPANY: POLYGRAM RECORDS ART DIRECTOR/DESIGNER: ETSUKO ISEKI DIGITAL ILLUSTRATION: SANJAY KOTHARI DESIGN FIRM: IN HOUSE PERFORMING ARTIST: HERBIE HANCOCK ALBUM TITLE: DIS IS DA DRUM ■ (OPPOSITE PAGE BOTTOM RIGHT) RECORD COMPANY: VERVE RECORDS/ POLYGRAM RECORDS ART DIRECTOR/DESIGNER/ILLUSTRATOR: LISA PO-YING HUANG DESIGN FIRM: IN-HOUSE PERFORMING ARTISTS: STUFF SMITH, DIZZY GILLESPIE, OSCAR PETERSON ALBUM TITLE: STUFF SMITH DIZZY GILLESPIE OSCAR PETERSON ■ (ABOVE) RECORD COMPANY: VERVE RECORDS/POLYGRAM RECORDS ART DIRECTOR/DESIGNER: CHRIS THOMPSON ILLUSTRATOR: JEFFERY FULUIMARI PERFORMING ARTIST: ELLA FITZGERALD ALBUM TITLE: THE COMPLETE ELLA FITZGERALD SONG BOOK

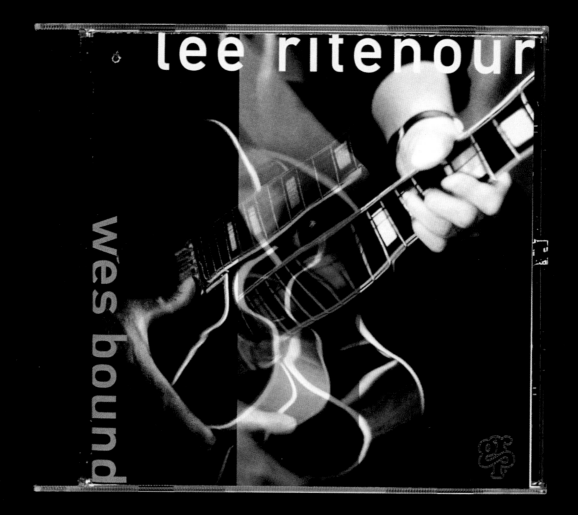

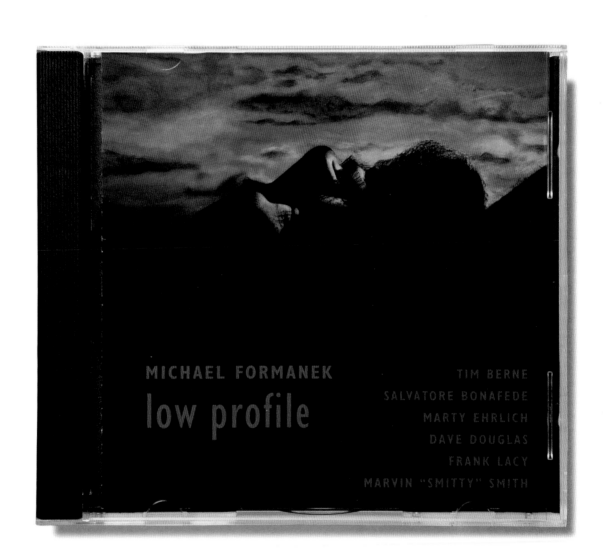

MICHAEL FORMANEK

low profile

TIM BERNE
SALVATORE BONAFEDE
MARTY EHRLICH
DAVE DOUGLAS
FRANK LACY
MARVIN "SMITTY" SMITH

(OPPOSITE PAGE) RECORD COMPANY: GRP RECORDS CREATIVE DIRECTOR: ANDY BALTIMORE DESIGNER: MARGO CHASE PHOTOGRAPHER: JOHN CASADO PERFORMING ARTISTS: LEE RITENOUR, WES MONTGOMERY ALBUM TITLE: WES BOUND ■ (THIS PAGE) RECORD COMPANY: ENJA RECORDS ART DIRECTOR/DESIGNER/PHOTOGRAPHER: SANDRA EISNER PERFORMING ARTIST: MICHAEL FORMANEK ALBUM TITLE: LOW PROFILE

RECORD COMPANY: COLUMBIA/LEGACY
ART DIRECTOR/DESIGNER: RISA ZAITSCHEK
ILLUSTRATOR: CALEF BROWN
DESIGN FIRM: SONY MUSIC
PERFORMING ARTIST: JOHNNY NASH
ALBUM TITLE: THE REGGAE COLLECTION

RECORD COMPANY: SONY MUSIC
ART DIRECTOR/DESIGNER: ALLEN WEINBERG
PHOTOGRAPHER: TIMOTHY WHITE
PERFORMING ARTIST: JIMMY CLIFF
ALBUM TITLE: HANGING FIRE

(ABOVE) RECORD COMPANY: © 1991 WARNER BROS. RECORDS ART DIRECTOR: JERI HEIDEN DESIGNER: SARAJO FRIEDEN PHOTOGRAPHER: PHILLIP DIXON DESIGN FIRM: WARNER BROS. IN-HOUSE ART DEPT. PERFORMING ARTIST: SHEILA E ALBUM TITLE: SEX CYMBAL ■ (OPPOSITE) RECORD COMPANY: MCA RECORDS ART DIRECTOR: VARTAN DESIGNER/ILLUSTRATOR: MICHAEL DIEHL PERFORMING ARTISTS: VARIOUS ALBUM TITLE: CHESS BLUES, 1–4

RECORD COMPANY: SONY MUSIC
ART DIRECTOR: TONY SELLARI
DESIGNER: C.M.O.N.
ALBUM TITLES: THE BEST OF...

RECORD COMPANY: MCA RECORDS
ART DIRECTOR: VARTAN
DESIGNER: JOHN O'BRIEN
PERFORMING ARTIST: B.B. KING
ALBUM TITLE: KING OF THE BLUES

RECORD COMPANY: ATLANTIC RECORDS
ART DIRECTOR: CAROL BOBOLTS
PHOTOGRAPHER: ROBIN NEDBOY
PERFORMING ARTISTS: VARIOUS
ALBUM TITLE: ATLANTIC BLUES CHICAGO

RECORD COMPANY: SONY MUSIC

ART DIRECTOR: ALLEN WEINBERG

DESIGNER: ALLEN WEINBERG

PERFORMING ARTIST: COLOR SCHEME

ALBUM TITLE: COLOR SCHEME

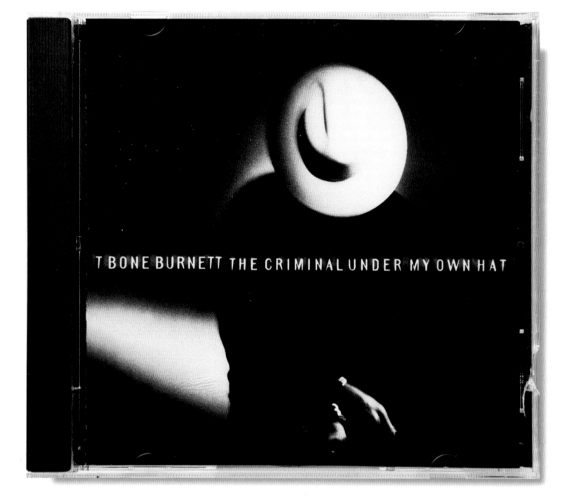

RECORD COMPANY: COLUMBIA RECORDS
ART DIRECTOR: MARY MAURER
PHOTOGRAPHER: STEVEN NILSSON
DESIGN FIRM: SONY MUSIC CREATIVE SERVICES
PERFORMING ARTIST: T BONE BURNETT
ALBUM TITLE: THE CRIMINAL UNDER MY OWN HAT

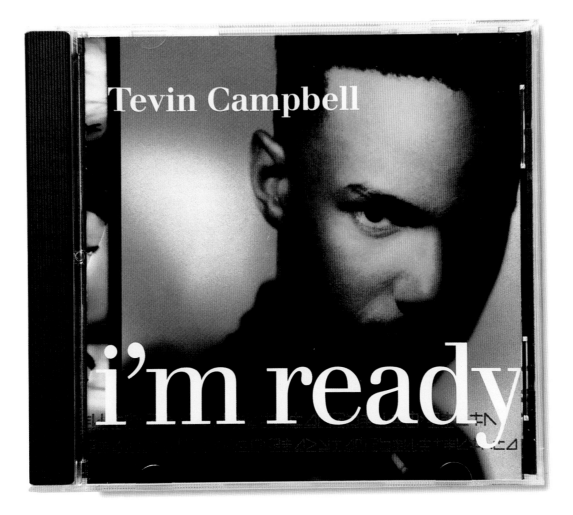

RECORD COMPANY: © 1993 QWEST RECORDS/WEA INTERNATIONAL INC.

ART DIRECTOR/DESIGNER: GREG ROSS

PHOTOGRAPHER: F. SCOTT SCHAFER

DESIGN FIRM: WARNER BROS. IN-HOUSE ART DEPARTMENT

PERFORMING ARTIST: TEVIN CAMPBELL

ALBUM TITLE: I'M READY

(OPPOSITE) RECORD COMPANY: KUDOS MUSIC ART DIRECTOR/DESIGNER: HARRY PEARCE DESIGN FIRM: LIPPA PEARCE DESIGN PERFORMING ARTIST: STEVE HACKETT ALBUM TITLE: BLUES WITH A FEELING ■ (ABOVE) RECORD COMPANY: CAPRICORN RECORDS ART DIRECTOR: KIM CHAMPAGNE DESIGNERS: KIM CHAMPAGNE, MICHAEL DIEHL ILLUSTRATOR: JOSH GOSFIELD PHOTOGRAPHER: GEORGE ADINS, COURTESY OF ROBERT SACRE DESIGN FIRM: WARNER BROS. IN-HOUSE ART DEPT. PERFORMING ARTIST: ELMORE JAMES ALBUM TITLE: KING OF THE SLIDE GUITAR

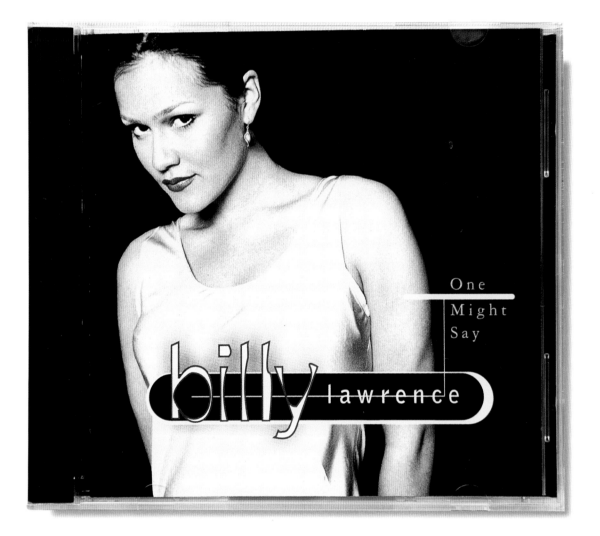

One
Might
Say

billy lawrence

RECORD COMPANY: EAST WEST RECORDS
ART DIRECTOR/DESIGNER: THOMAS BRICKER
PHOTOGRAPHER: DANIEL HASTINGS
PERFORMING ARTIST: BILLY LAWRENCE
ALBUM TITLE: ONE MIGHT SAY

One
Might
Say

billy lawrence

1. One Might Say (4:27)
2. Feelings Carry On (4:41)
3. Happiness (4:14)
4. Truly (4:34)
5. Boyfriend (5:04)
6. Favorite One (4:23)
7. My Heart My Angel (4:33)
8. Prelude (0:35)
9. Your Good Luv (4:12)
10. Distant Love (5:21)
11. Good Times & Bad (4:56)
12. Forgive Me Baby (6:23)
13. I'm In A Daze (4:02)

92367-2

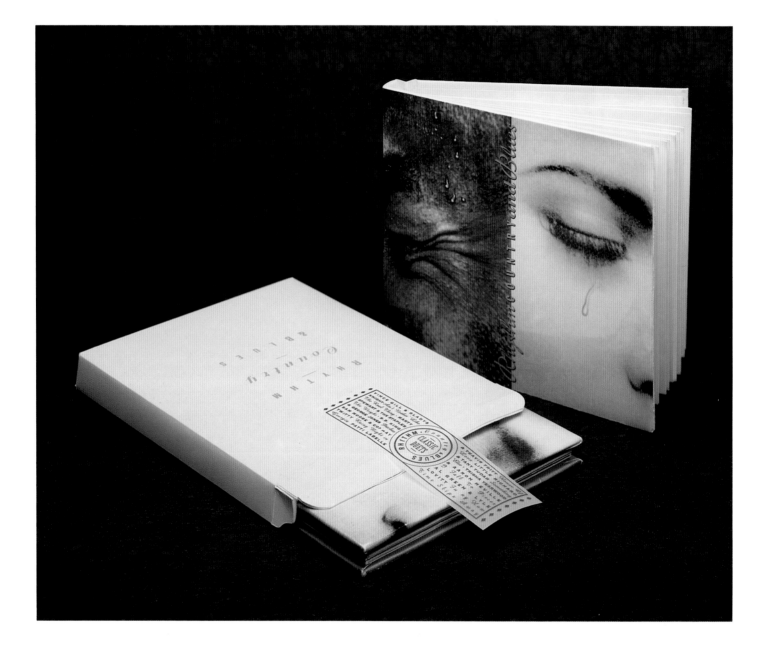

(THIS PAGE) RECORD COMPANY: MCA RECORDS ART DIRECTOR: VARTAN DESIGNER: ANDY ENGEL ILLUSTRATOR: ANDY ENGEL PERFORMING ARTISTS: VARIOUS ALBUM TITLE: RHYTHM, COUNTRY & BLUES ■ (OPPOSITE PAGE) RECORD COMPANY: MCA RECORDS ART DIRECTOR: VARTAN DESIGNER: MICHAEL DIEHL ILLUSTRATOR: MICHAEL DIEHL PERFORMING ARTISTS: VARIOUS ALBUM TITLE: CHESS BLUES

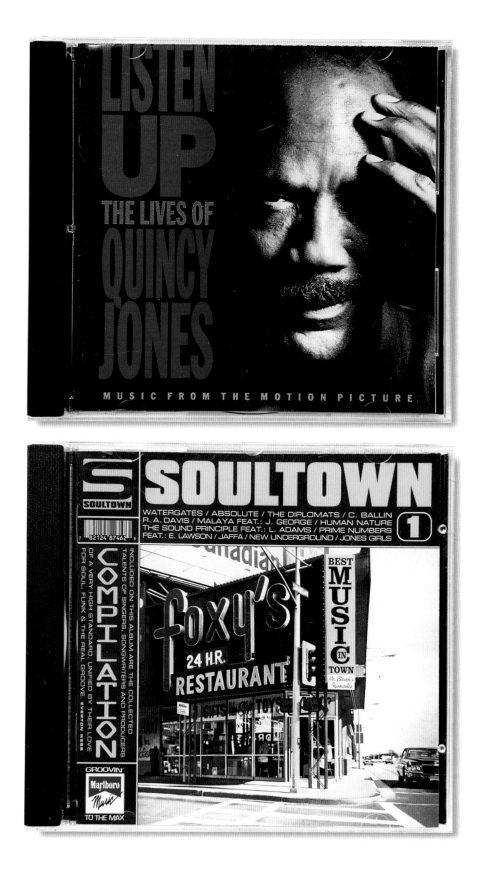

(THIS SPREAD TOP ROW) Record Company: WARNER BROS. RECORDS Design Firm: FRANKFURT GIPS BALKIND Photographer: PATRICK DEMARCHELIER Performing Artist: QUINCY JONES Album Title: LISTEN UP: THE LIVES OF QUINCY JONES ■ (THIS SPREAD BOTTOM

ROW) Record Company: MARLBORO MUSIC Art Director: HANS HAMMERS, JR. II Designers: HANS HAMMERS JR. II , WOLFGANG VON GERAMB Illustrator: MICHAEL MAU Design Firm: HEADCHARGE Performing Artist: SOULTOWN Album Title: COMPILATIONS

(THIS SPREAD)
RECORD COMPANY: SONY MUSIC
ART DIRECTOR/DESIGNER: MARK BURDETT
PHOTOGRAPHER: FRANK W. OCKENFELS
PERFORMING ARTIST/ALBUM TITLE: KEB' MO

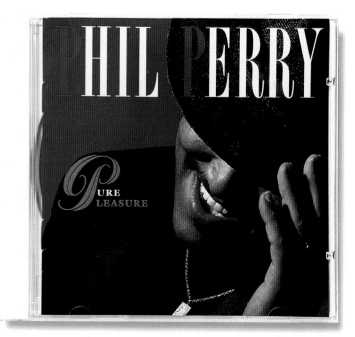

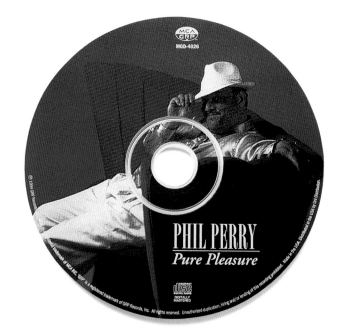

(OPPOSITE TOP) RECORD COMPANY: GRP RECORDS ART DIRECTOR: HOLLIS KING, DAN SERRANO DESIGNERS: LAURIE GOLDMAN, ALBA ACEVEDO, FREDDIE PALOMA PHOTOGRAPHER: CAROL WEINBERG PERFORMING ARTIST: PHIL PERRY ALBUM TITLE: PURE PLEASURE ■ (OPPOSITE CENTER LEFT) RECORD COMPANY: ISLAND RECORDS ART DIRECTOR: TONY WRIGHT DESIGNER: ALDO SAMPIERI PHOTOGRAPHER: MICHAEL LAVINE PERFORMING ARTIST: BUCKWHEAT ZYDECO ALBUM TITLE: FIVE CARD STUD ■ (OPPOSITE CENTER RIGHT) RECORD

COMPANY: SONY MUSIC ART DIRECTOR: TONY SELLARI DESIGNER: C.M.O.N. PERFORMING ARTIST: THE O'JAYS ALBUM TITLE: THE O'JAYS IN PHILADELPHIA ■ (OPPOSITE BOTTOM LEFT AND RIGHT) RECORD COMPANY: MCA RECORDS ART DIRECTOR: VARTAN DESIGNER/ILLUSTRATOR: ANDY ENGEL PERFORMING ARTISTS: VARIOUS ALBUM TITLE: RHYTHM, COUNTRY & BLUES ■ (THIS PAGE) RECORD COMPANY: RHINO RECORDS ART DIRECTOR: COCO SHINOMIYA DESIGNER: RACHEL GUTEK PERFORMING ARTISTS: VARIOUS ALBUM TITLE: THE SUN RECORDS COLLECTION

(THIS PAGE) RECORD COMPANY: LUAKA BOP RECORDS/WARNER BROS. DESIGNERS: DAVID BYRNE, DOUBLESPACE NY DESIGN FIRM: DOUBLESPACE NY PERFORMING ARTIST: DAVID BYRNE ALBUM TITLE: REI MOMO ■ (OPPOSITE) RECORD COMPANY: CAPITOL RECORDS ART DIRECTOR: NORMAN MOORE DESIGNER: NORMAN MOORE DESIGN FIRM: DESIGN ART INC. PERFORMING ARTIST: HEART ALBUM TITLE: BRIGADE ■ (FOLLOWING SPREAD, LEFT PAGE TOP ROW) RECORD COMPANY: LUAKA BOP/RECORDS/WARNER BROS. ART DIRECTOR: GABRIELLE RAUMBERGER DESIGNER: GEGGY TAH ILLUSTRATOR/COMPUTER IMAGING: DYLAN TRAN PHOTOGRAPHERS: TOMMY JORDAN, MARINA CHAVEZ, GREG KURSTIN, CRAIG CURRIE DESIGN FIRM: GABRIELLE RAUMBERGER DESIGN PERFORMING ARTIST: GEGGY TAH ALBUM TITLE: GRAND OPENING ■ (FOLLOWING SPREAD LEFT PAGE SECOND ROW) RECORD COMPANY: FUGATA LTD. ART DIRECTOR: MARGUS HAAVAMÄGI DESIGNER: MARGUS HAAVAMÄGI PHOTOGRAPHER: MARGUS HAAVAMÄGI PERFORMING ARTIST: SAXAPPEAL ALBUM TITLE:

OH LADY BE COOL ■ (FOLLOWING SPREAD LEFT PAGE THIRD ROW) RECORD COMPANY: CASCOT MUSIC ART DIRECTOR: STEVEN SANDSTROM DESIGNER: STEVEN SANDSTROM PHOTOGRAPHER: C.B. HARDING DESIGN FIRM: SANDSTROM DESIGN PERFORMING ARTIST: SMOKE AND MIRRORS ALBUM TITLE: CARRY A MASK ■ (FOLLOWING SPREAD LEFT PAGE BOTTOM ROW) RECORD COMPANY: ELEKTRA RECORDS ART DIRECTOR: GABRIELLE RAUMBERGER DESIGNER: DYLAN TRAN PHOTOGRAPHER: CHARLES STEELE DESIGN FIRM: GABRIELLE RAUMBERGER DESIGN PERFORMING ARTIST: THE EAGLES ALBUM TITLE: THE VERY BEST OF THE EAGLES ■ (FOLLOWING SPREAD RIGHT PAGE TOP ROW) RECORD COMPANY: BARKING PUMPKIN ART DIRECTOR: FRANK ZAPPA DESIGNERS: BRIAN JOHNSON, JESSE DI FRANCO PHOTOGRAPHERS: FRITZ BRINCKMANN (COVER), HENNING LOHNER, HANS JÖRG MICHEL DESIGN FIRM: COMMAND A STUDIOS PERFORMING ARTIST: FRANK ZAPPA ALBUM TITLE: THE YELLOW SHARK ENSEMBLE MODERN ■ (FOLLOWING SPREAD RIGHT PAGE SECOND ROW)

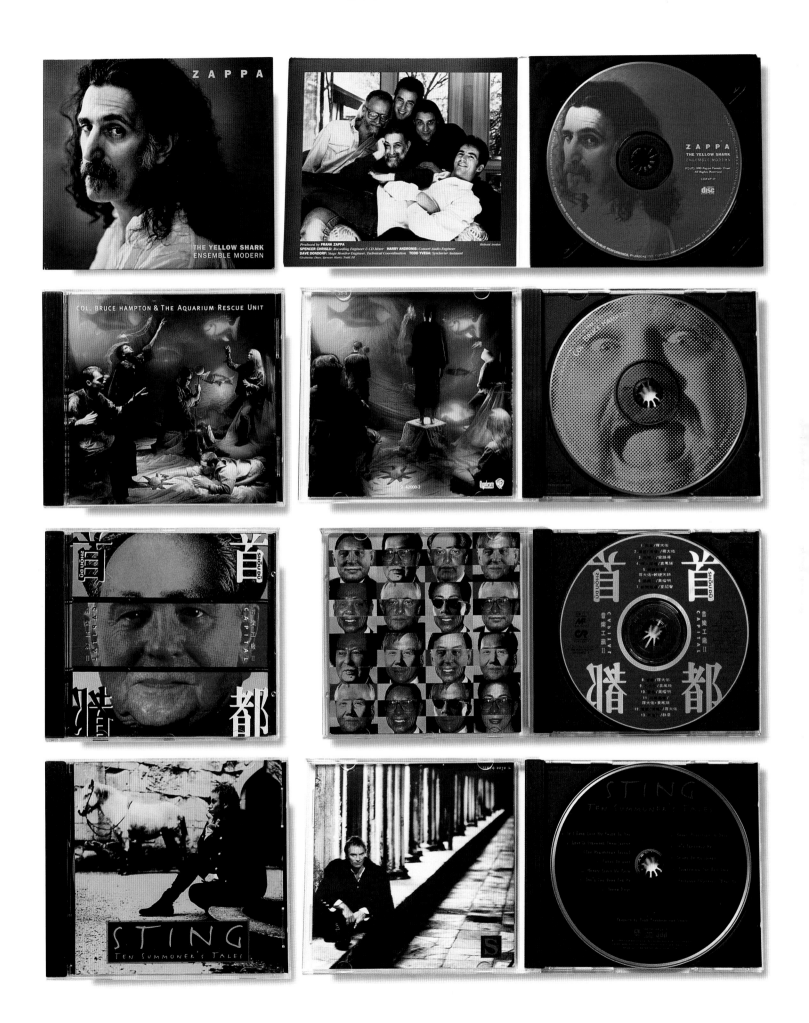

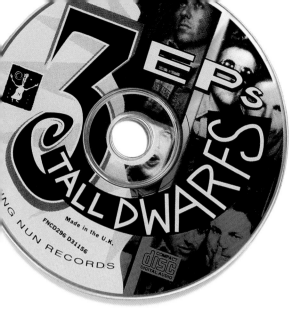

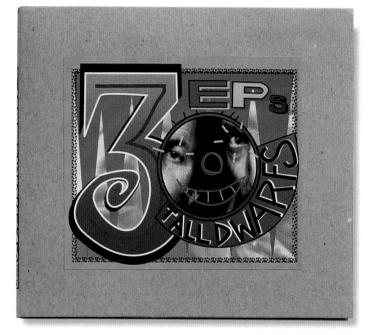

RECORD COMPANY: CAPRICORN RECORDS ART DIRECTOR: MARCIA BEVERLY DESIGNER: DEBORAH NORCROSS PHOTOGRAPHER: JEFF FRAZIER PERFORMING ARTIST: COL. BRUCE HAMPTON & THE AQUARIUM RESCUE UNIT ALBUM TITLE: COL. BRUCE HAMPTON & THE AQUARIUM RESCUE UNIT ■ (PRECEDING SPREAD RIGHT PAGE THIRD ROW) RECORD COMPANY: MUSIC FACTORY ART DIRECTOR: ALAN CHAN DESIGNERS: ALAN CHAN, PETER LO DESIGN FIRM: ALAN CHAN DESIGN COMPANY PERFORMING ARTISTS: VARIOUS ALBUM TITLE: SHOU DU ■ (PRECEDING SPREAD RIGHT PAGE BOTTOM ROW) RECORD COMPANY: A&M RECORDS ART DIRECTORS: RICHARD FRANKEL, NORMAN

MOORE DESIGNERS: RICHARD FRANKEL, NORMAN MOORE PHOTOGRAPHER: KEVIN WESTENBERG DESIGN FIRMS: A&M RECORDS IN-HOUSE, DESIGN ART INC. PERFORMING ARTIST: STING ALBUM TITLE: TEN SUMMONER'S TALES ■ (OPPOSITE CORNER AND LEFT AND THIS PAGE BOT-TOM) RECORD COMPANY: FLYING NUN RECORDS DESIGNERS: ALEC BATHGATE, CHRIS KNOX PERFORMING ARTIST: TALL DWARFS ALBUM TITLE: 3 EPS ■ (OPPOSITE PAGE RIGHT AND THIS PAGE TOP) RECORD COMPANY: CECI-CELÀ/VIRGIN FRANCE DESIGNER: GÉRARD LO MONACO (METAL BOX) ILLUSTRATORS: GÉRARD LO MONACO, FRÉDÉRIC RÉBÉNA PERFORMING ARTIST: RENAUD ALBUM TITLE: LA BELLE DE MAI

(THIS PAGE) RECORD COMPANY: ELEKTRA RECORDS ART DIRECTOR: LAURIE HENZEL DESIGNER: LAURIE HENZEL PHOTOGRAPHER: MICHAEL LAVINE PERFORMING ARTIST: LUNA ALBUM TITLE: BEWITCHED ■ (OPPOSITE PAGE) RECORD COMPANY: NORMAL RECORDS ART DIRECTORS: KERSTIN VIEG, OLAF MEYER DESIGNER: OLAF MEYER PHOTOGRAPHER: KERSTIN VIEG PERFORMING ARTIST: MYRNA LOY ALBUM TITLE: TIME SAYS HELAY ■ (FOLLOWING SPREAD TOP ROW) RECORD COMPANY: MCA RECORDS ART DIRECTORS: TIM STEDMAN DESIGNER: DAVID HIGH ILLUSTRATOR: MARK DURHAM DESIGN FIRM: HIGH DESIGN PERFORMING ARTISTS: VARIOUS ALBUM TITLE: MUSCLE ■

(FOLLOWING SPREAD CENTER ROW) RECORD COMPANY: MCA RECORDS ART DIRECTOR: VARTAN DESIGNER: JOHN COULTER PHOTOGRAPHER: ALBERT WATSON PERFORMING ARTIST: BOBBY BROWN ALBUM TITLE: BOBBY ■ (FOLLOWING SPREAD BOTTOM ROW) RECORD COMPANY: COLUMBIA RECORDS ART DIRECTOR: MARY MAURER ILLUSTRATOR: JASON HOLLEY TYPE/LETTERING: JASON HOLLEY TYPE ASSISTANCE: STEVEN SALARDINO PHOTOGRAPHER: MICHAEL WILSON PERFORMING ARTIST: TOAD THE WET SPROCKET ALBUM TITLE: DULCINEA

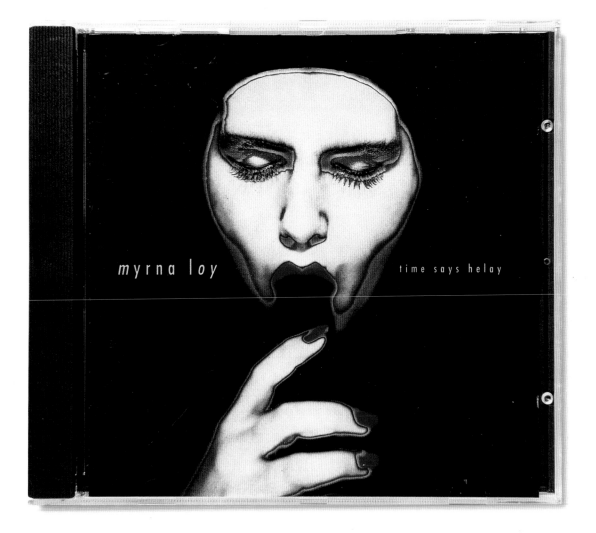

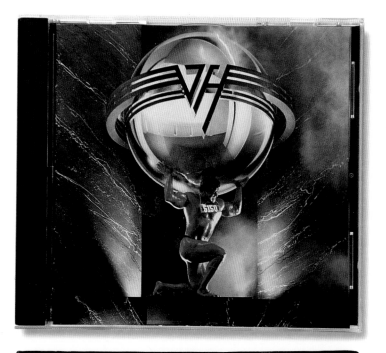

(PRECEDING SPREAD TOP) RECORD COMPANY: WARNER BROS. RECORDS ART DIRECTOR: JERI MCMANUS PHOTOGRAPHER: AARON RAPOPORT PERFORMING ARTIST: VAN HALEN ALBUM TITLE: 5150 ■ (PRECEDING SPREAD CENTER) RECORD COMPANY: © 1990 SIRE RECORDS/ WEA INTERNATIONAL ART DIRECTORS: TOM RECCHION, SYLVIA REED DESIGNERS: TOM RECCHION, SYLVIA REED PHOTOGRAPHER: JAMES HAMILTON DESIGN FIRM: WARNER BROS. IN-HOUSE ART DEPARTMENT PERFORMING ARTISTS: LOU REED, JOHN CALE ALBUM TITLE: SONGS FOR DRELLA ■ (PRECEDING SPREAD BOTTOM) RECORD COMPANY: © 1993 QWEST RECORDS ART DIRECTORS: JEFF GOLD, STEPHEN BAKER,

PETER SAVILLE DESIGNERS: PETER SAVILLE, BRETT WICKENS, HOWARD WAKEFIELD DESIGN FIRM: PENTAGRAM, LONDON PERFORMING ARTIST: NEW ORDER ALBUM TITLE: REPUBLIC ■ (ABOVE) RECORD COMPANY: © 1990 GIANT RECORDS ART DIRECTORS/DESIGNERS: JERI HEIDEN, DEBORAH NORCROSS PHOTOGRAPHER: HENRY DILTZ DESIGN FIRM: WARNER BROS. IN-HOUSE ART DEPARTMENT PERFORMING ARTIST: HINDU LOVE GODS ALBUM TITLE: HINDU LOVE GODS ■ (OPPOSITE) RECORD COMPANY: WARNER BROS. RECORDS ART DIRECTOR: BOB SEIDEMAN ILLUSTRATOR: JOHN VAN HAMMERSVELD PERFORMING ARTIST: GRATEFUL DEAD ALBUM TITLE: SKELETONS FROM THE CLOSET

(THIS PAGE) RECORD COMPANY: © 1993 CAPRICORN RECORDS/WEA INTERNATIONAL ART DIRECTOR/DESIGNER: DEBORAH NORCROSS ILLUSTRATORS: HENK ELENGA (COVER LOGO AND LOGO), ERIC STOTIC (FRONT COVER) PHOTOGRAPHERS: MELODIE MCDANIEL (BAND), PAUL CAPONIGRO (SUNFLOWER), ALASTAIR THAIN (HAND) DESIGN FIRM: WARNER BROS. IN-HOUSE ART DEPARTMENT PERFORMING ARTIST: 311 ALBUM TITLE: MUSIC ■ (OPPOSITE TOP) RECORD COMPANY: © 1993 WARNER BROS. RECORDS/WEA INTERNATIONAL ART DIRECTOR/DESIGNER: DEBORAH NORCROSS PHOTOGRAPHER: MERLYN ROSENBERG DESIGN FIRM: WARNER BROS. IN-HOUSE ART DEPARTMENT PERFORMING ARTIST: JANE CHILD ALBUM TITLE: HERE NOT THERE ■ (OPPOSITE SECOND ROW) RECORD COMPANY: © 1993 WARNER BROS. RECORDS ART DIRECTOR: GEORGE DESIGNER: DEBORAH NORCROSS PHOTOGRAPHER: FRANK LUTEREC DESIGN FIRM: WARNER BROS. IN-HOUSE ART DEPARTMENT

PERFORMING ARTIST: GOO GOO DOLLS ALBUM TITLE: SUPERSTAR CAR WASH ■ (OPPOSITE THIRD ROW) RECORD COMPANY: © 1989 WARNER BROS. RECORDS/WEA INTERNATIONAL INC. ART DIRECTORS/DESIGNERS: ELVIS COSTELLO, JERI HEIDEN LOGO DESIGNER: JOHN HEIDEN MODEL MAKING: LIZARD STUDIO PHOTOGRAPHER: BRIAN GRIFFIN DESIGN FIRM: WARNER BROS. IN-HOUSE ART DEPARTMENT PERFORMING ARTIST: ELVIS COSTELLO ALBUM TITLE: SPIKE ■ (OPPOSITE BOTTOM) RECORD COMPANY: © 1994 WARNER BROS. RECORDS/WEA INTERNA-TIONAL ART DIRECTOR/DESIGNER: KIM CHAMPAGNE ILLUSTRATOR: RICH HUELGA PHOTOGRAPHER: MIKE HASHIMOTO COVER IMAGE: *VAGABOND* DESIGN FIRM: WARNER BROS. IN-HOUSE ART DEPARTMENT PERFORMING ARTIST: BIOHAZARD ALBUM TITLE: STATE OF THE WORLD ADDRESS

(THIS PAGE TOP ROW) RECORD COMPANY: © 1990 REPRISE RECORDS/WEA INTERNATIONAL ART DIRECTOR/DESIGNER: JERI HEIDEN HAND LETTERING: LARIMIE GARCIA ILLUSTRATOR: MARK RYDEN PHOTOGRAPHER: MICHAEL WILSON DESIGN FIRM: WARNER BROS. IN-HOUSE ART DEPT PERFORMING ARTIST: 3RD MATINEE ALBUM TITLE: MEANWHILE ■ (THIS PAGE BOTTOM ROW) RECORD COMPANY: GIANT RECORDS ART DIRECTOR/DESIGNER: DEBORAH NORCROSS IDEOQUE TYPEFACE DESIGN: MICHAEL DIEHL PHOTOGRAPHERS: ANTHONY ARTIAGA, MELODIE MCDANIEL

DESIGN FIRM: WARNER BROS. IN-HOUSE ART DEPT PERFORMING ARTIST/ALBUM TITLE: BOINGO ■ (OPPOSITE) RECORD COMPANY: © 1993 WARNER BROS. RECORDS ART DIRECTOR: JERI HEIDEN DESIGNERS: JERI HEIDEN, LYN BRADLEY PHOTOGRAPHERS: DAVID GRAHAM (FRONT AND BACK COVER), JOHN HALPERN (LIVE SHOTS), SAMANTHA HARVEY, ROBERT BUHL, MARK SELIGER (STILL BAND SHOTS) DESIGN FIRM: WARNER BROS. IN-HOUSE ART DEPT. PERFORMING ARTIST: VAN HALEN ALBUM TITLE: VAN HALEN LIVE: RIGHT HERE, RIGHT NOW

RECORD COMPANY: WARNER BROS. RECORDS. © 1990 PAUL SIMON
ART DIRECTORS/DESIGNERS: JERI HEIDEN (PACKAGE), YOLANDA CUOMO (BOOKLET)
PHOTOGRAPHER: SYLVIA PLACHY
DESIGN FIRM: WARNER BROS. IN-HOUSE ART DEPARTMENT
PERFORMING ARTIST: PAUL SIMON
ALBUM TITLE: THE RHYTHM OF THE SAINTS

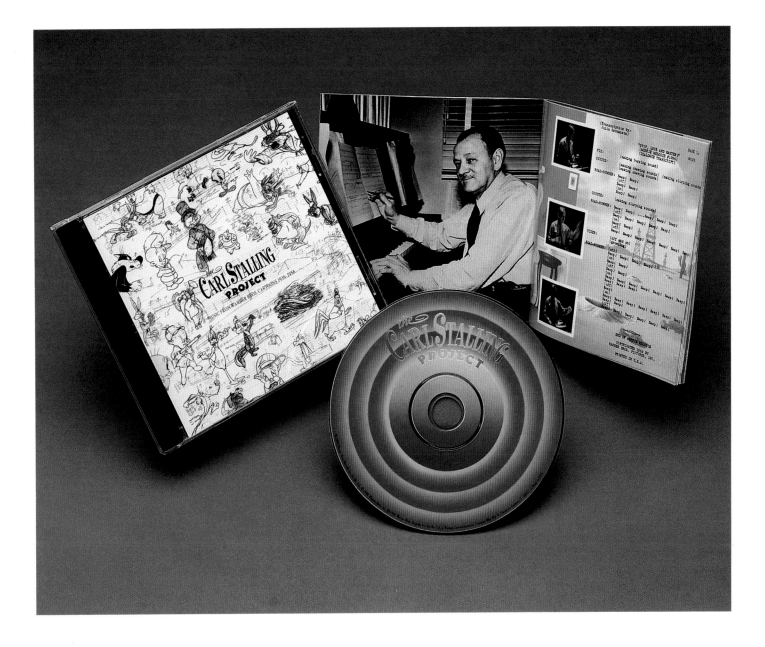

RECORD COMPANY: © 1990 WARNER BROS. RECORDS/WEA INTERNATIONAL

ART DIRECTOR/DESIGNER: TOM RECCHION

PHOTOGRAPHY/ILLUSTRATION: WARNER BROS. ANIMATION ARCHIVES, STEVE SCHNIEDER ARCHIVES

DESIGN FIRM: WARNER BROS. IN-HOUSE ART DEPARTMENT

PERFORMING ARTIST: THE CARL STALLING PROJECT

ALBUM TITLE: MUSIC FROM WARNER BROTHERS CARTOONS 1936–1958

(THIS PAGE) RECORD COMPANY: © 1990 REPRISE RECORDS/WEA INTERNATIONAL ART DIRECTORS: JERI HEIDEN, DEBORAH NORCROSS DESIGNER: DEBORAH NORCROSS PHOTOGRAPHER: ALASTAIR THAIN DESIGN FIRM: WARNER BROS. IN-HOUSE ART DEPARTMENT PERFORMING ARTIST: TOY MATINEE ALBUM TITLE: TOY MATINEE ■ (OPPOSITE PAGE TOP) RECORD COMPANY: © 1991 GIANT RECORDS ART DIRECTOR:

DEBORAH NORCROSS DESIGNER: DEBORAH NORCROSS PHOTOGRAPHER: MERLYN ROSENBERG DESIGN FIRM: WARNER BROS. IN-HOUSE ART DEPT PERFORMING ARTIST: HOUSE OF FREAKS ALBUM TITLE: CAKEWALK ■ (OPPOSITE BOTTOM) RECORD COMPANY: REPRISE RECORDS/WARNER BROS. RECORDS ART DIRECTORS: JANET LEVINSON, JOEL BERNSTEIN DESIGNER: JANET LEVINSON PHOTOGRAPHER: JOEL BERNSTEIN DESIGN FIRM: WARNER BROS. IN-HOUSE ART DEPT PERFORMING ARTIST: NEIL YOUNG ALBUM TITLE: HARVEST MOON

(OPPOSITE) RECORD COMPANY: © 1991 SLASH RECORDS ART DIRECTOR: KIM CHAMPAGNE PHOTOGRAPHER: STUART WATSON PERFORMING ARTIST: BODEANS ALBUM TITLE: BLACK AND WHITE ■ (ABOVE) RECORD COMPANY: WARNER BROS. RECORDS ART DIRECTORS: TOM RECCHION, MICHAEL STIPE PHOTOGRAPHER: ANTON CORBIJN DESIGN FIRM: WARNER BROS. ART DEPT PERFORMING ARTIST: R.E.M. ALBUM TITLE: LOSING MY RELIGION

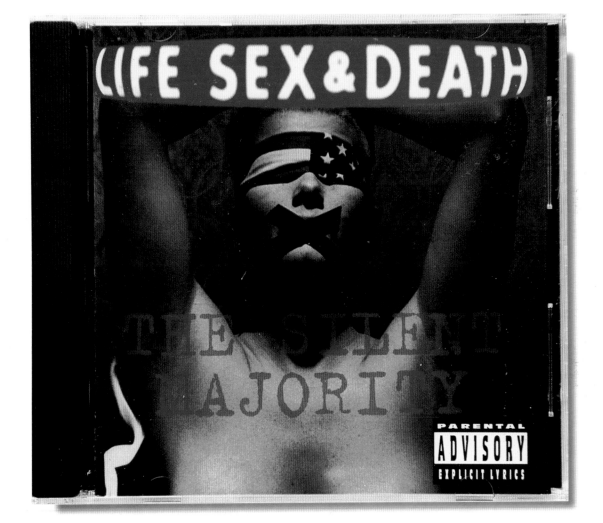

(OPPOSITE PAGE) RECORD COMPANY: © SLASH RECORDS ART DIRECTORS: TOM RECCHION, LOUIE PEREZ PHOTOGRAPHER: DENNIS KEELEY DESIGN FIRM: WARNER BROS. ART DEPARTMENT PERFORMING ARTIST: LOS LOBOS ALBUM TITLE: KIKO ■ (THIS PAGE) RECORD COMPANY: © 1992 REPRISE RECORDS/WEA INTERNATIONAL INC. ART DIRECTOR: DEBORAH NORCROSS DESIGNERS: DEBORAH NORCROSS, P. SCOTT MAKELA, LIFE, SEX AND DEATH LOGOTYPE: P. SCOTT MAKELA PHOTOGRAPHER: AMY GUIP DESIGN FIRM: WARNER BROS. ART DEPARTMENT PERFORMING ARTIST: LIFE, SEX AND DEATH ALBUM TITLE: THE SILENT MAJORITY

(OPPOSITE) RECORD COMPANY: © 1989 THE DAVID GEFFEN COMPANY ART DIRECTOR/DESIGNER: JERI HEIDEN DESIGN FIRM: WARNER BROS. IN-HOUSE ART DEPARTMENT PERFORMING ARTIST: DON HENLEY ALBUM TITLE: END OF THE INNOCENCE ■ (THIS PAGE TOP LEFT) RECORD COMPANY: © 1993 WARNER BROS. RECORDS/WEA INTERNATIONAL INC. ART DIRECTOR: JERI HEIDEN DESIGNER: JERI HEIDEN PHOTOGRAPHER: JAN SAUDEK DESIGN FIRM: WARNER BROS. IN-HOUSE ART DEPARTMENT PERFORMING ARTIST: DANIEL LANOIS ALBUM TITLE: FOR THE BEAUTY OF WYNONA ■ (THIS PAGE TOP RIGHT) RECORD COMPANY: © 1990 SIRE RECORDS/WEA INTERNATIONAL ART DIRECTOR: KIM CHAMPAGNE,

MICHAEL REY DESIGNERS: MICHAEL REY, GREG LINDY PHOTOGRAPHER: MICHAEL WILSON DESIGN FIRMS: WARNER BROS. IN-HOUSE ART DEPT, REY INT'L PERFORMING ARTIST: THE REPLACEMENTS ALBUM TITLE: ALL SHOOK DOWN ■ (BOTTOM LEFT) RECORD COMPANY: © 1989 SIRE RECORDS/ WEA INTERNATIONAL ART DIRECTOR: JERI HEIDEN DESIGNER: JERI HEIDEN LOGO DESIGN: MARGO CHASE PHOTOGRAPHER: HERB RITTS DESIGN FIRM: WARNER BROS. IN-HOUSE ART DEPT. PERFORMING ARTIST: MADONNA ALBUM TITLE: LIKE A PRAYER ■ (BOTTOM RIGHT) RECORD COMPANY: © 1991 REPRISE RECORDS/WEA INTERNATIONAL ART DIRECTOR: KIM CHAMPAGNE DESIGNER: KIM CHAMPAGNE PHOTOGRAPHER: ANNALISA PESSIN DESIGN FIRM: WARNER BROS. IN-HOUSE ART DEPT. PERFORMING ARTIST: ADAM SCHMITT ALBUM TITLE: WORLD SO BRIGHT

(OPPOSITE TOP) RECORD COMPANY: © 1992 WARNER BROS. RECORDS CREATIVE DIRECTOR: SOTERA TSCHETTER ART DIRECTORS: JEFF GOLD, GREG ROSS DESIGNERS: JEFF GOLD, GREG ROSS, LIZ LUCE HANDLETTERING: LORNA STOVALL EYE LOGO: MIKE DIEHL PHOTOGRAPHER: JEFF KATZ DESIGN FIRM: WARNER BROS. IN-HOUSE ART DEPT. PERFORMING ARTIST: PRINCE AND THE NEW POWER GENERATION ALBUM TITLE: (SYMBOL) ■

(BOTTOM) RECORD COMPANY: © 1991 REPRISE RECORDS ART DIRECTORS: JEFF GOLD, KIM CHAMPAGNE DESIGNER: KIM CHAMPAGNE PHOTOGRAPHER: ENRIQUE BALDELESCU DESIGN FIRM: WARNER BROS. IN-HOUSE ART DEPT PERFORMING ARTIST: SQUEEZE ALBUM TITLE: PLAY ■ (THIS PAGE) RECORD COMPANY: © 1990 SIRE RECORDS/WEA INTERNATIONAL ART DIRECTOR: JERI HEIDEN DESIGNERS: JERI HEIDEN, JOHN HEIDEN PHOTOGRAPHER: HERB RITTS DESIGN FIRM: WARNER BROS. IN-HOUSE ART DEPT. PERFORMING ARTIST: MADONNA ALBUM TITLE: THE ROYAL BOX

(THIS PAGE) RECORD COMPANY: © 1993 REPRISE RECORDS ART DIRECTOR: JERI HEIDEN DESIGNERS: JERI HEIDEN, LYN BRADLEY PAINTINGS: TIM LOWLEY PHOTOGRAPHER: FLORA SIGISMONDI DESIGN FIRM: WARNER BROS. IN-HOUSE ART DEPARTMENT PERFORMING

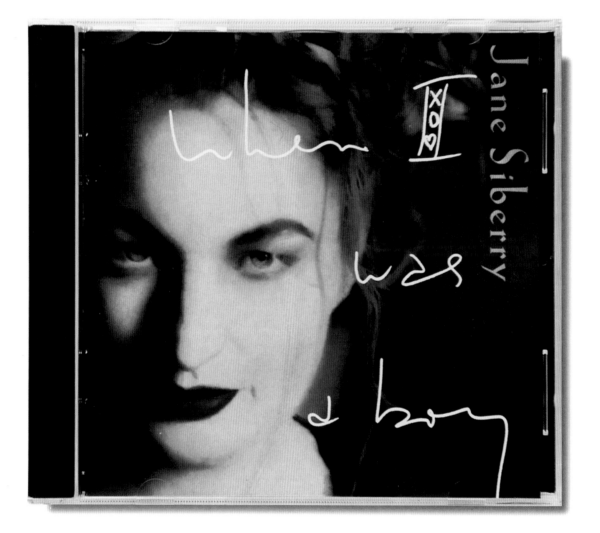

ARTIST: JAN SIBERRY ALBUM TITLE: WHEN I WAS A BOY ■ (OPPOSITE PAGE) RECORD COMPANY: © 1993 QWEST RECORDS ART DIRECTOR: TOM RECCHION DESIGNER: TOM RECCHION COMPUTER IMAGING: TOM RECCHION PERFORMING ARTIST: NEW ORDER ALBUM TITLE: IN ORDER

NEW ORDER
IN ORDER

(TOP) RECORD COMPANY: ROLLING STONES RECORDS/VIRGIN RECORDS ART DIRECTOR/DESIGNER: PETER CORRISTON ILLUSTRATOR: CHRISTIAN PIPER PERFORMING ARTIST: THE ROLLING STONES ALBUM TITLE: TATTOO YOU ■ (BOTTOM) RECORD COMPANY: VIRGIN RECORDS ART DIRECTOR/DESIGNER: LEN PELTIER PHOTOGRAPHER: PATRICK DEMARCHELIER PERFORMING ARTIST: JANET JACKSON ALBUM TITLE: JANET

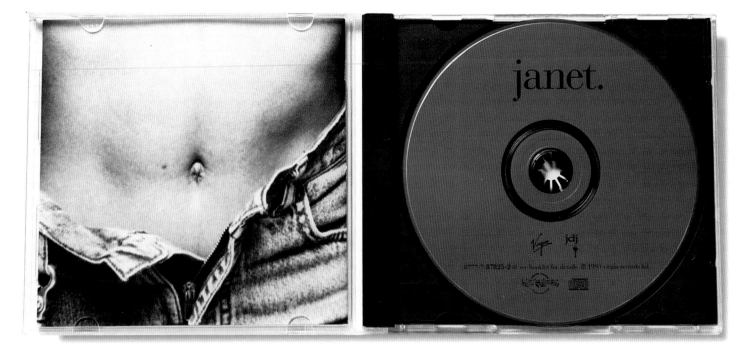

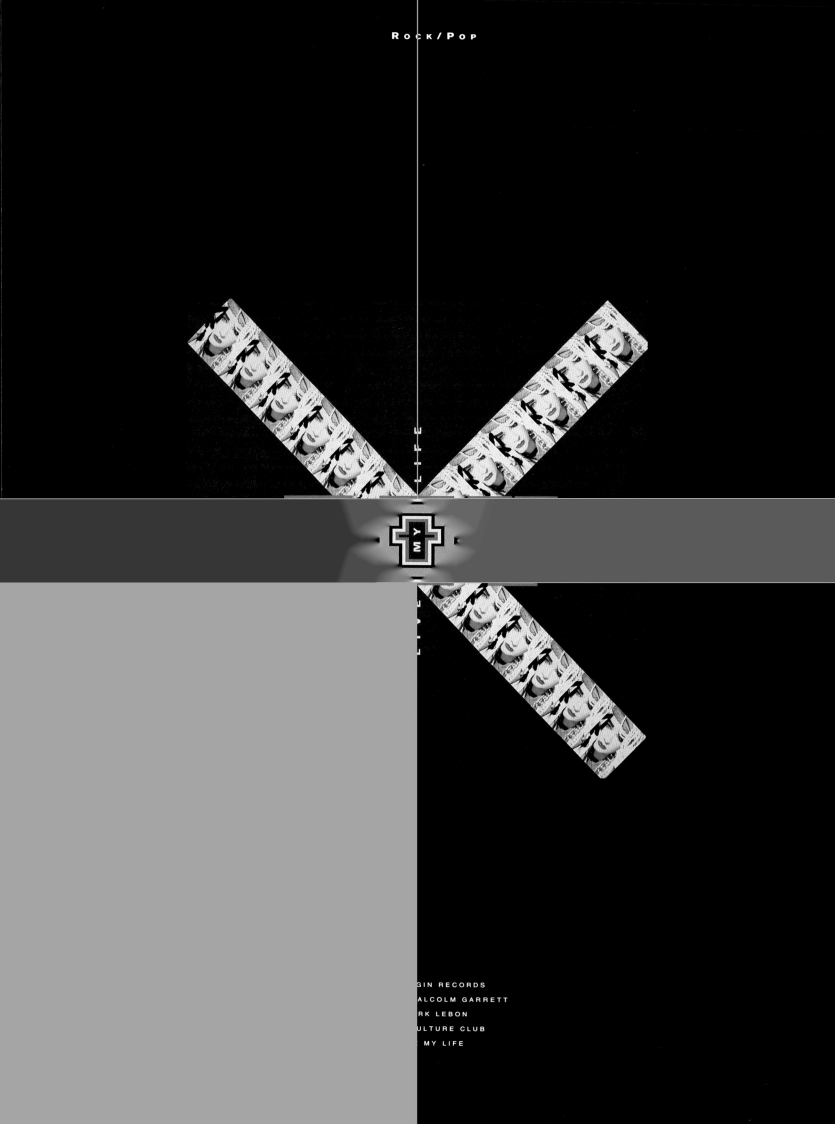

DESIGNER: MALCOLM GARRETT

PHOTOGRAPHERS: MARK LEBON, DAVID LEVINE, JAMIE MORGAN

PERFORMING ARTIST: CULTURE CLUB

ALBUM TITLE: THIS TIME

RECORD COMPANY: VIRGIN RECORDS
DESIGNER: MALCOLM GARRETT
PHOTOGRAPHERS: MARK LEBON, DAVID LEVINE, JAMIE MORGAN
PERFORMING ARTIST: CULTURE CLUB
ALBUM TITLE: THIS TIME

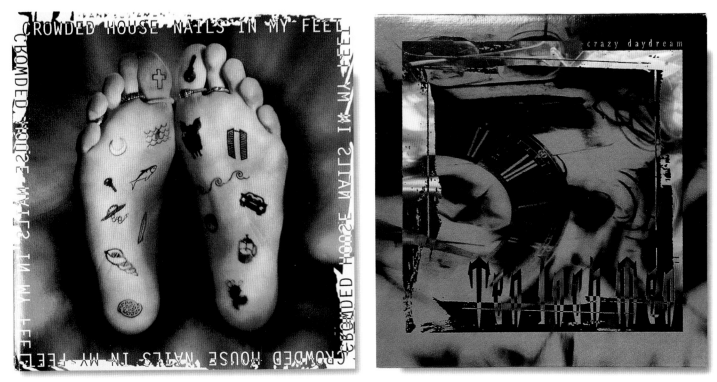

(OPPOSITE) RECORD COMPANY: CAPITOL RECORDS ART DIRECTOR: MARGO CHASE DESIGNER: ANNE BURDICK PHOTOGRAPHER: SIDNEY COOPER DESIGN FIRM: MARGO CHASE DESIGN PERFORMING ARTIST: CROWDED HOUSE ALBUM TITLE: PRIVATE UNIVERSE ■ (ABOVE TOP LEFT) RECORD COMPANY: CAPITOL RECORDS ART DIRECTOR/DESIGNER: MARGO CHASE ILLUSTRATOR: NICK SEYMOUR PHOTOGRAPHER: MERLYN ROSENBERG DESIGN FIRM: MARGO CHASE DESIGN PERFORMING ARTIST: CROWDED HOUSE ALBUM TITLE: NAILS IN MY FEET ■ (TOP RIGHT) RECORD COMPANY: VICTORY MUSIC ART DIRECTOR/DESIGNER: MARGO CHASE PHOTOGRAPHER: MERLYN ROSENBERG DESIGN FIRM: MARGO CHASE DESIGN PERFORMING ARTIST: TEN INCH MEN ALBUM TITLE: CRAZY DAY DREAM ■ (BOTTOM LEFT) RECORD COMPANY: CAPITOL RECORDS ART DIRECTOR: MARGO CHASE DESIGNER: ANNE BURDICK PHOTOGRAPHER: MERLYN ROSENBERG DESIGN FIRM: MARGO CHASE DESIGN PERFORMING ARTIST: CROWDED HOUSE ALBUM TITLE: LOCKED OUT ■ (BOTTOM RIGHT) RECORD COMPANY: VICTORY MUSIC, INC. ART DIRECTOR/DESIGNER: MARGO CHASE PHOTOGRAPHER: MERLYN ROSENBERG DESIGN FIRM: MARGO CHASE DESIGN PERFORMING ARTIST: TEN INCH MEN ALBUM TITLE: PRETTY

(OPPOSITE TOP) RECORD COMPANY: WARNER BROS. RECORDS ART DIRECTOR: KIM CHAMPAGNE DESIGNER: MARGO CHASE PHOTOGRAPHER: SIDNEY COOPER DESIGN FIRM: MARGO CHASE DESIGN PERFORMING ARTIST: RENAISSANCE ALBUM TITLE: TALES OF 1001 NIGHTS ■ (OPPOSITE BOTTOM) RECORD COMPANY: VIRGIN RECORDS ART DIRECTOR: MELANIE NISSEN DESIGNER: MARGO CHASE PHOTOGRAPHER: ROBERT

LOBETTA DESIGN FIRM: MARGO CHASE DESIGN PERFORMING ARTIST: PAULA ABDUL ALBUM TITLE: SPELLBOUND ■ (THIS PAGE) RECORD COMPANY: GEFFEN RECORDS ART DIRECTORS: ROBIN SLOANE, SAMANTHA HART DESIGNER/ILLUSTRATOR: MARGO CHASE PHOTOGRAPHERS: HERB RITTS, MERLYN ROSENBERG DESIGN FIRM: MARGO CHASE DESIGN PERFORMING ARTIST: CHER ALBUM TITLE: LOVE HURTS

RECORD COMPANY: CHRYSALIS RECORDS
DESIGNERS: MICHAEL • NASH ASSOCIATES, KARL WALLINGER
PERFORMING ARTIST: WORLD PARTY
ALBUM TITLE: GOODBYE JUMBO

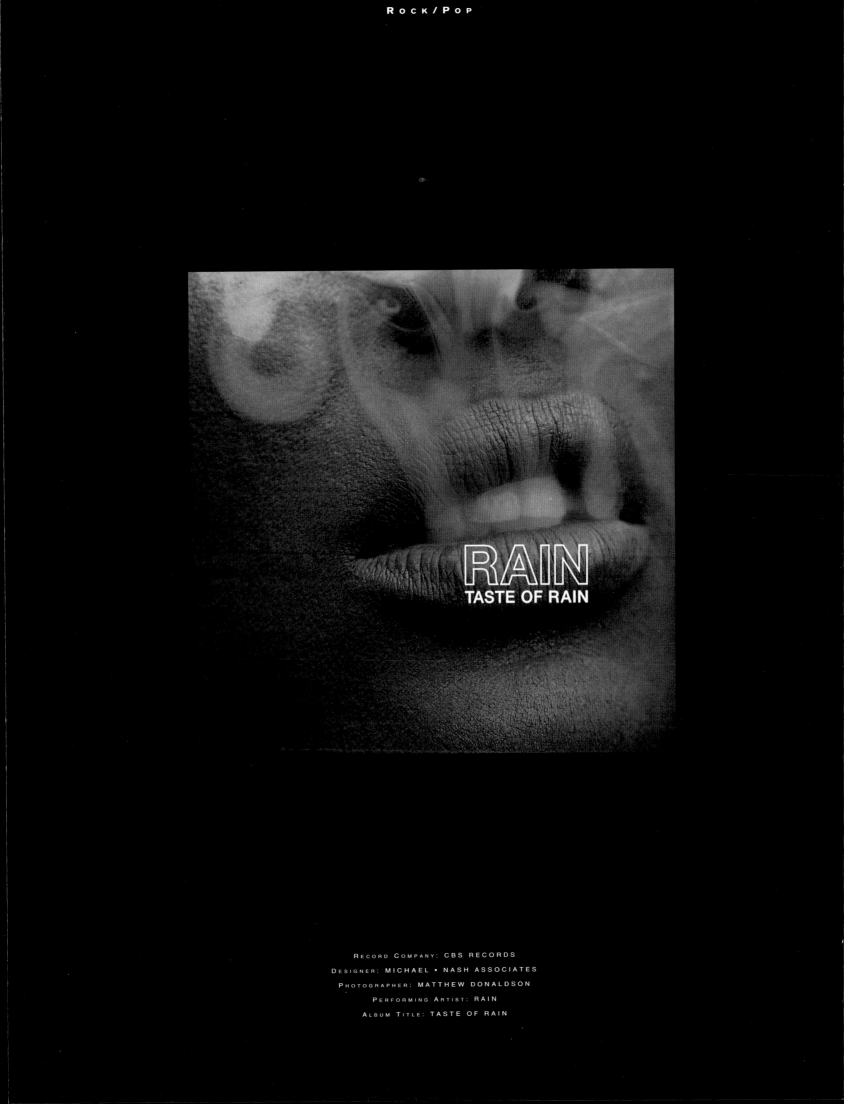

RECORD COMPANY: CBS RECORDS
DESIGNER: MICHAEL • NASH ASSOCIATES
PHOTOGRAPHER: MATTHEW DONALDSON
PERFORMING ARTIST: RAIN
ALBUM TITLE: TASTE OF RAIN

(THIS PAGE) Record Company: LEGACY RECORDS Art Director: NICKY LINDEMAN Performing Artist: JEFF BECK Album Title: BECKOLOGY ■ (OPPOSITE PAGE) Record Company: BMG ARIOLA Art Directors: CHRISTINA KRUTZ, THOMAS SASSENBACH Designer: CHRISTINA KRUTZ Illustrator: CHRISTINA KRUTZ Design Firm: CHRISTINA KRUTZ DESIGN Album Title: SCHÄRFEN SIE IHRE SINNE

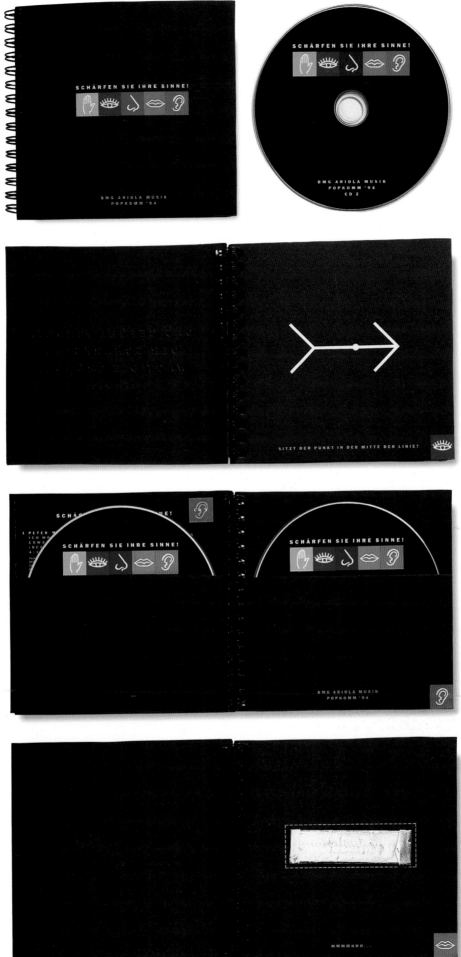

(THIS PAGE TOP) RECORD COMPANY: SPV RECORDS DESIGNER/PHOTOGRAPHER: SABINE POTTHAST PERFORMING ARTIST: DOUBLE KEY ALBUM
TITLE: LIFE IS IN THE RHYTHM ■ (THIS PAGE BOTTOM) RECORD COMPANY: SPV RECORDS DESIGNER: SABINE POTTHAST PERFORMING ARTIST:
REX ALBUM TITLE: DINOS IN THE PARK ■ (OPPOSITE) RECORD COMPANY: NORMAL RECORDS ART DIRECTORS: KERSTIN VIEG, OLAF MEYER
DESIGNER: OLAF MEYER PHOTOGRAPHER: KERSTIN VIEG PERFORMING ARTIST: LOUIS TILLETT ALBUM TITLE: LETTERS TO A DREAM

(THIS PAGE TOP LEFT) RECORD COMPANY: SPV RECORDS DESIGNER: ULLI PFLEGER PHOTOGRAPHER: BERNHARD KÜHMSTEDT PERFORMING ARTIST: CAROLYNE MAS ALBUM TITLE: REASON STREET ■ (THIS PAGE TOP RIGHT) RECORD COMPANY: SPV RECORDS DESIGNER: SABINE POTTHAST PHOTOGRAPHER: BERNHARD KÜHMSTEDT PERFORMING ARTIST: CAROLYNE MAS ALBUM TITLE: DRIVING ON THE RADIO ■ (THIS PAGE BOTTOM LEFT) RECORD COMPANY: SPV RECORDS DESIGNER: SABINE POTTHAST PHOTOGRAPHER: SABINE POTTHAST PERFORMING ARTIST: BAD DAYS IN JUNE ALBUM TITLE: WELCOME TO A BRAND NEW DAY ■ (THIS PAGE BOTTOM RIGHT) RECORD COMPANY: SPV RECORDS DESIGNER: SABINE POTTHAST PERFORMING ARTIST: BAD DAYS IN JUNE ALBUM TITLE: EYES CLOSED ■ (OPPOSITE) RECORD COMPANY: SPV RECORDS DESIGNER: SABINE POTTHAST PERFORMING ARTIST: PLASTIC BERTRAND ALBUM TITLE: CA PLANE POUR MOI

(THIS SPREAD)

RECORD COMPANY: CHRYSALIS RECORDS

ART DIRECTOR/DESIGNER: EDDIE DEIGHTON

PERFORMING ARTIST: KINGMAKER

ALBUM TITLE: 10 YEARS ASLEEP

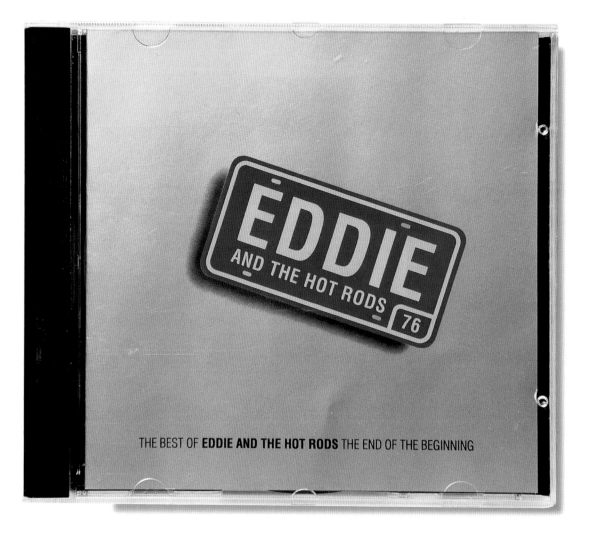

RECORD COMPANY: SONY MUSIC
ART DIRECTOR/DESIGNER: VINCE FROST
DESIGN FIRM: FROST DESIGN
PERFORMING ARTISTS: EDDIE AND THE HOT RODS
ALBUM TITLE: THE END OF THE BEGINNING

RECORD COMPANY: GEFFEN RECORDS
ART DIRECTORS: ROBIN SLOANE, JANET WOLSBORN
PHOTOGRAPHER: DAVID SKERNICK
PERFORMING ARTIST: EAGLES
ALBUM TITLE: HELL FREEZES OVER

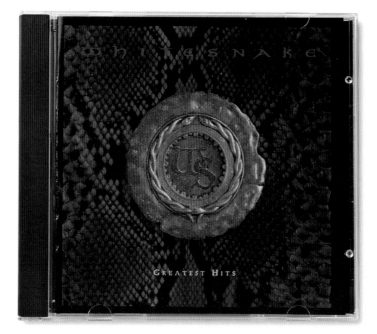

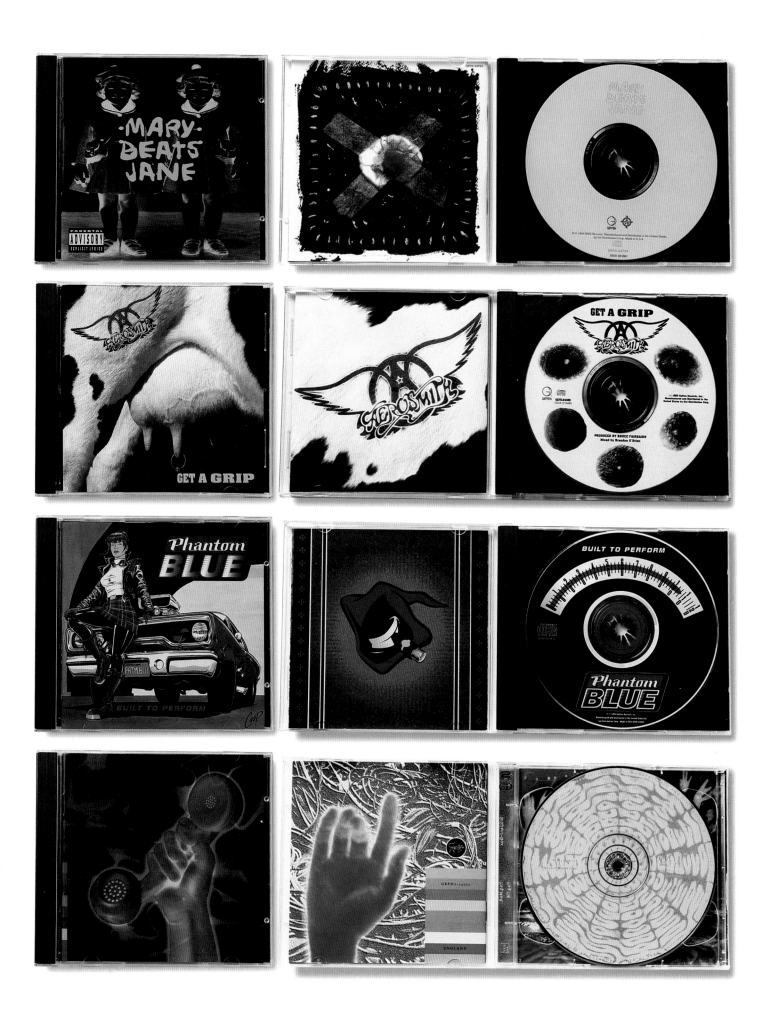

(PAGES 156, 157 TOP ROW) RECORD COMPANY: GEFFEN RECORDS ART DIRECTOR: HUGH SYME DESIGNER: HUGH SYME ILLUSTRATOR: HUGH SYME PERFORMING ARTIST: TESLA ALBUM TITLE: BUST A NUT ■ (PAGES 156, 157 CENTER ROW) RECORD COMPANY: GEFFEN RECORDS ART DIRECTOR: MALCOLM GARRETT PHOTOGRAPHER: DAVID SCHEINMANN PERFORMING ARTIST: PETER GABRIEL ALBUM TITLE: US ■ (PAGES 156, 157 BOTTOM ROW) RECORD COMPANY: GEFFEN RECORDS ART DIRECTOR/DESIGNER: HUGH SYME PHOTOGRAPHER: BERNARD BOUDREAU PERFORMING ARTIST: WHITESNAKE ALBUM TITLE: WHITESNAKE'S GREATEST HITS ■ (PAGE 158 TOP ROW) RECORD COMPANY: GEFFEN RECORDS ART DIRECTOR/DESIGNER: ANDRÉ HINDERSSON PHOTOGRAPHY: BLACK BOX PERFORMING ARTIST/ALBUM TITLE: MARY BEATS JANE ■ (PAGE 158 SECOND ROW) RECORD COMPANY: GEFFEN RECORDS ART DIRECTOR: MICHAEL GOLOB DESIGNER: HUGH SYME PERFORMING ARTIST: AEROSMITH ALBUM TITLE: GET A GRIP ■ (PAGE 158 THIRD ROW) RECORD COMPANY: GEFFEN RECORDS ART DIRECTOR: MICHAEL GOLOB DESIGNER: MICHAEL GOLOB ILLUSTRATOR: CHRIS COOPER PHOTOGRAPHER: RAUL VEGA PERFORMING ARTIST: PHANTOM BLUE ALBUM TITLE: BUILT TO PERFORM ■ (PAGE 158 BOTTOM ROW) RECORD COMPANY: GEFFEN RECORDS ART DIRECTOR: MICHAEL COULSON DESIGNER: TONY STILES COVER IMAGES: DANNY JENKINS, FAB 4 PHOTOGRAPHER: STEPHEN LOVELL-DAVIS PERFORMING ARTIST: PETER GABRIEL ALBUM TITLE: SECRET WORLD LIVE ■ (PAGE 159 TOP ROW) RECORD COMPANY: GEFFEN RECORDS ART DIRECTOR/DESIGNER: ROBERT FISHER PHOTOGRAPHERS: KIRK WEDDLE, MICHAEL LAVINE PERFORMING ARTIST: NIRVANA ALBUM TITLE: NEVERMIND ■ (PAGE 159 SECOND ROW) RECORD COMPANY: GEFFEN RECORDS ART DIRECTOR/DESIGNER: ROBERT FISHER PHOTOGRAPHER: MICHAEL LAVINE PERFORMING ARTIST: URGE OVERKILLL ALBUM TITLE:

SATURATION ■ (PAGE 159 THIRD ROW) RECORD COMPANY: GEFFEN RECORDS CREATIVE DIRECTOR: ROBIN SLOANE ART COORDINATION: SOFIE HOWARD ART DIRECTOR: MARYLYNNE BARBIS DESIGNER: MARYLYNNE BARBIS PHOTOGRAPHER: MICHAEL HALSBAND DESIGN FIRM: BARBIS & RASKE PERFORMING ARTIST/ALBUM TITLE: PRIDE & GLORY ■ (PAGE 159 BOTTOM ROW) RECORD COMPANY: GEFFEN RECORDS ART DIRECTOR: FRANK OLINSKY COVER PAINTING: PAL SHAZAR PHOTOGRAPHER: JOHN HARDIN PERFORMING ARTIST: THE WATERBOYS ALBUM TITLE: DREAM HARDER ■ (THIS PAGE LEFT) RECORD COMPANY: COLUMBIA RECORDS ART DIRECTOR: JOSEPHINE DIDONATO PHOTOGRAPHER: PHILIP DIXION PERFORMING ARTIST: MARIAH CAREY ALBUM TITLE: EMOTIONS ■ (THIS PAGE RIGHT) RECORD COMPANY: SONY MUSIC ART DIRECTOR: CHRISTOPHER AUSTOPCHUK DESIGNER: JUNE HONG PHOTOGRAPHER: LISA HAUN PERFORMING ARTISTS: LUTHER VANDROSS & MARIAH CAREY ALBUM TITLE: ENDLESS LOVE ■ (OPPOSITE TOP) RECORD COMPANY: CAPRICORN RECORDS ART DIRECTOR: DEBORAH NORCROSS DESIGNER: LESLIE WINTNER PHOTOGRAPHER: JEFF FRAZIER PERFORMING ARTIST: COL. BRUCE HAMPTON & THE AQUARIUM RESCUE UNIT ALBUM TITLE: MIRRORS OF EMBARRASSMENT ■ (OPPOSITE PAGE CENTER) RECORD COMPANY: CAPRICORN RECORDS ART DIRECTORS: MARCIA BEVERLY, KIMBERLIN BROWN DESIGNER: ALLISON CORLEW PHOTOGRAPHER: LESLEY BOHM PERFORMING ARTIST: DIXIE DREGS ALBUM TITLE: FULL CIRCLE ■ (OPPOSITE BOTTOM) RECORD COMPANY: © 1990 WARNER BROS. RECORDS/WEA INTERNATIONAL ART DIRECTOR: PERRY FARRELL DESIGNERS: TOM RECCHION, KIM CHAMPAGNE ILLUSTRATORS: PERRY AND CASEY PHOTOGRAPHER: VICTOR BRACKE DESIGN FIRM: WARNER BROS. IN-HOUSE ART DEPARTMENT PERFORMING ARTIST: JANE'S ADDICTION ALBUM TITLE: RITUAL DE LO HABITUAL

1 NO EGO'S UNDER WATER 2 LOST MY MULE IN TEXAS 3 IT'S NOT THE SAME OLD THING 4 TOO MANY GUITARS 5 GONE TODAY, HERE TOMORROW 6 SHOELESS JOE 7 LIVES OF LONGEVITY 8 MEMORY IS A GIMMICK 9 DEAD PRESIDENTS 10 TRONDOSSA 11 SWING 12 PAYDAY

COL. BRUCE HAMPTON & THE AQUARIUM RESCUE UNIT
MIRRORS OF EMBARRASSMENT

DIXIE DREGS
FULL CIRCLE

DIXIEDREGSFULLCIRCLE
PRODUCED BY STEVE MORSE
℗© 1994 Capricorn Records. All rights reserved. Dist. by RED. 42021-2

JANE'S ADDICTION
RITUAL DE LO HABITUAL

(OPPOSITE PAGE) RECORD COMPANY: GEFFEN RECORDS ART DIRECTOR: HUGH SYME DESIGNER: HUGH SYME PERFORMING ARTIST: COVERDALE/PAGE ALBUM TITLE: COVERDALE • PAGE ■ (THIS PAGE TOP) RECORD COMPANY: GEFFEN RECORDS ART DIRECTOR: ROBERT FISHER DESIGNER: ROBERT FISHER PHOTOGRAPHERS: ROSS HARRIS, JOHN SKALICKY PERFORMING ARTIST: BECK ALBUM TITLE: MELLOW GOLD ■ (THIS PAGE BOTTOM) RECORD COMPANY: GEFFEN RECORDS ART DIRECTOR: JANET WOLSBORN DESIGNER: JANET WOLSBORN PHOTOGRAPHER: LENDON FLANAGAN PERFORMING ARTISTS: LYLE MAYS, MARC JOHNSON, JACK DEJOHNETTE ALBUM TITLE: FICTIONARY

(THIS PAGE TOP) RECORD COMPANY: GEFFEN RECORDS ART DIRECTOR/DESIGNER: MICHAEL GOLOB ILLUSTRATOR: SHEIK PHOTOGRAPHER: ALISON DYER PERFORMING ARTIST: JACKYL ALBUM TITLE: PUSH COMES TO SHOVE ■ (THIS PAGE BOTTOM) RECORD COMPANY: GEFFEN RECORDS ART DIRECTOR: JANET WOLSBORN COVER PAINTING: EDIE BRICKELL PERFORMING ARTIST: EDIE BRICKELL ALBUM TITLE: PICTURE PERFECT MORNING ■ (OPPOSITE PAGE) RECORD COMPANY: GEFFEN RECORDS ART DIRECTORS: KIM CHAMPAGNE, GABRIELLE RAUMBERGER ILLUSTRATOR: MARK RYDEN PHOTOGRAPHER: NORMAN SEEFF PERFORMING ARTIST: AEROSMITH ALBUM TITLE: PUMP

(THIS PAGE LEFT) RECORD COMPANY: GEFFEN RECORDS ART DIRECTOR: KEVIN REAGAN PHOTOGRAPHER: DENNIS KEELEY PERFORMING
ARTIST/ALBUM TITLE: NOA ■ (THIS PAGE RIGHT) RECORD COMPANY: GEFFEN/DGC RECORDS ART DIRECTOR: MICHAEL GOLOB DESIGNER:
KARL KOCH PHOTOGRAPHER: PETER GOWLAND PERFORMING ARTIST: WEEZER ALBUM TITLE: WEEZER ■ (OPPOSITE TOP) RECORD COMPANY:
GEFFEN RECORDS ART DIRECTORS/DESIGNERS: LAURIE HENZEL, CELL COVER PAINTING: RODRIGO ALIVA PHOTOGRAPHER: MARK C. DESIGN
FIRM: HENZEL DESIGN PERFORMING ARTIST: CELL ALBUM TITLE: LIVING ROOM ■ (OPPOSITE PAGE CENTER LEFT) RECORD COMPANY:

GEFFEN RECORDS ART DIRECTOR: KEVIN REAGAN DESIGNER: JANET WOLSBORN ILLUSTRATOR: JEFFREY VALLANCE PHOTOGRAPHER:
DENNIS KEELEY PERFORMING ARTIST: PETER CASE ALBUM TITLE: SIX-PACK OF LOVE ■ (OPPOSITE PAGE CENTER RIGHT) RECORD
COMPANY: GEFFEN RECORDS ART DIRECTOR: GABRIELLE RAUMBERGER DESIGNERS: GABRIELLE RAUMBERGER, LYN BRADLEY
ILLUSTRATOR: KOHLENE HENDRICKSON PHOTOGRAPHERS: DENNIS KEELEY, MICHAEL LAVINE PERFORMING ARTIST: NELSON ALBUM TITLE:
AFTER THE RAIN ■ (OPPOSITE PAGE BOTTOM) RECORD COMPANY: GEFFEN/DGC RECORDS ART DIRECTORS: KURT COBAIN, ROBERT
FISHER DESIGNERS: KURT COBAIN, ROBERT FISHER ILLUSTRATOR: ALEX GREY PERFORMING ARTIST: NIRVANA ALBUM TITLE: IN UTERO

(THIS PAGE TOP) RECORD COMPANY: GEFFEN RECORDS CREATIVE DIRECTOR: ROBIN SLOANE ART DIRECTOR: WENDY SHERMAN DESIGNER: WENDY SHERMAN PHOTOGRAPHER: STUART WATSON PERFORMING ARTIST: BLUE MURDER ALBUM TITLE: NOTHIN' BUT TROUBLE ■ (THIS PAGE BOTTOM) RECORD COMPANY: GEFFEN RECORDS ART DIRECTOR: MARYLYNNE BARBIS PHOTOGRAPHER: E.J. CAMP DESIGN FIRM: BARBIS & RASKE PERFORMING ARTIST: SAMMY HAGAR ALBUM TITLE: UNBOXED ■ (OPPOSITE PAGE) RECORD COMPANY: EPIC/COLUMBIA RECORDS ART DIRECTOR: RISA ZAITSCHEK DESIGNER: RISA ZAITSCHEK PHOTOGRAPHER: ROBERT LEWIS DESIGN FIRM: SONY MUSIC PERFORMING ARTISTS: VARIOUS ALBUM TITLE: STANLEY, SON OF THEODORE: YET ANOTHER ALTERNATIVE MUSIC SAMPLER

Stanley, Son of Theodore:
Yet Another Alternative Music Sampler

COMPACT disc DIGITAL AUDIO

1. **Senseless Things**
   Everybody's Gone†

2. **Big Audio Dynamite II**
   Kool-Aid (British Version)

3. **The Shamen**
   Make It Mine (Remix)†

4. **Manic Street Preachers**
   Love's Sweet Exile†*

5. **Sun-60**
   Out Of My Head

6. **Cypress Hill**
   Hand On The Pump *

7. **Pearl Jam**
   Alive (Live)

8. **Fishbone**
   Fight The Youth (Remix)

9. **Shabba Ranks**
   Woodtop (Non-Album Cut)

10. **Public Enemy**
    Nighttrain (Remix)

11. **Eye & I**
    Venus In Furs

12. **Bruce Cockburn**
    Kit Carson

13. **Indigo Girls**
    Pushing The Needle Too Far (Live)

14. **Poi Dog Pondering**
    Get Me On **

15. **Gregg Alexander**
    The Truth

16. **Alison Moyet**
    It Won't Be Long (Acoustic)†

0 7464-47304-2

AAD/*ADD/
**DAD/·DDD

COLUMBIA
epic
epic
Def Jam Recordings
RUFF HOUSE RECORDS

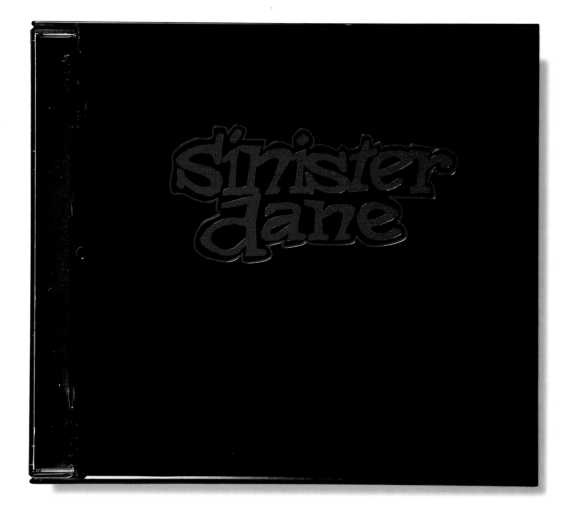

RECORD COMPANY: COLUMBIA RECORDS
ART DIRECTOR: JIM DEBARROS
DESIGNERS: JIM DEBARROS, TIM MANTEAU
PERFORMING ARTIST/ALBUM TITLE: SINISTER DANE

RECORD COMPANY: COLUMBIA RECORDS
ART DIRECTOR/DESIGNER: SARA ROTMAN
PERFORMING ARTIST: BILLY JOEL
ALBUM TITLE: SHADES OF GREY

(OPPOSITE TOP) RECORD COMPANY: EPIC RECORDS ART DIRECTOR/DESIGNER: CAROL CHEN PHOTOGRAPHER: AMY GUIP PERFORMING ARTIST: LIVING COLOUR ALBUM TITLE: STAIN ■ (OPPOSITE SECOND ROW) RECORD COMPANY: EPIC RECORDS ART DIRECTOR: CAROL CHEN DESIGNER: TRACEY BOYCHUCK PHOTOGRAPHER: KEN SCHLES PERFORMING ARTIST: PRONG ALBUM TITLE: CLEANSING ■ (OPPOSITE THIRD ROW AND ABOVE TOP) RECORD COMPANY: SONY MUSIC ART DIRECTOR/DESIGNER: SARA ROTMAN PERFORMING ARTISTS: VARIOUS ALBUM TITLE: JOY TO THE WORLD ■ (OPPOSITE BOTTOM ROW) RECORD COMPANY: SONY MUSIC ART DIRECTOR: JOSEPHINE DIDONATO PHOTOGRAPHER: DANIELA FEDERICI PERFORMING ARTIST: MARIAH CAREY ALBUM TITLE: MUSIC BOX ■ (BELOW) RECORD COMPANY: EPIC RECORDS ART DIRECTOR: JOEL ZIMMERMAN DESIGNERS: JEFF AMENT, JOEL ZIMMERMAN PHOTOGRAPHERS: JEFF AMENT, LANCE MERCER PERFORMING ARTIST/ALBUM TITLE: PEARL JAM

(OPPOSITE PAGE TOP LEFT) RECORD COMPANY: NORMAL RECORDS ART DIRECTORS: KERSTIN VIEG, OLAF MEYER DESIGNER: OLAF MEYER PHOTOGRAPHER: KERSTIN VIEG PERFORMING ARTIST: MELINDA MIEL ALBUM TITLE: THE LAW OF THE DREAM ■ (OPPOSITE TOP RIGHT) RECORD COMPANY: NORMAL RECORDS ART DIRECTORS: KERSTIN VIEG, OLAF MEYER DESIGNER: OLAF MEYER PHOTOGRAPHER: KERSTIN VIEG PERFORMING ARTIST: THE DUBROVNIKS ALBUM TITLE: AUDIO SONIC LOVE AFFAIR ■ (OPPOSITE CENTER LEFT) RECORD COMPANY: EPIC/550 MUSIC ART DIRECTOR: SARA ROTMAN DESIGNER: SARA ROTMAN PHOTOGRAPHER: JO ANN TOY PERFORMING ARTIST: EVE'S PLUM ALBUM TITLE: BLUE ■ (OPPOSITE PAGE CENTER RIGHT) RECORD COMPANY: COLUMBIA RECORDS ART DIRECTORS: ARNOLD LEVINE, JOSEPHINE

COSMIC PSYCHOS SLAVE TO THE CRAVE

Live at the Palace—Melbourne

DIDONATO PHOTOGRAPHER: DANIELA FEDERICI PERFORMING ARTIST: HARRY CONNICK, JR. ALBUM TITLE: SHE ■ (OPPOSITE PAGE BOTTOM LEFT) RECORD COMPANY: NORMAL RECORDS ART DIRECTORS: KERSTIN VIEG, OLAF MEYER DESIGNER: OLAF MEYER PHOTOGRAPHER: KERSTIN VIEG PERFORMING ARTIST: KASTRIERTE PHILOSOPHEN ALBUM TITLE: NERVES ■ (OPPOSITE BOTTOM RIGHT) RECORD COMPANY: NORMAL RECORDS ART DIRECTORS: KERSTIN VIEG, OLAF MEYER DESIGNER: OLAF MEYER PHOTOGRAPHER: KERSTIN VIEG PERFORMING ARTISTS: VARIOUS ALBUM TITLE: 10 JAHRE NORMAL ■ (THIS PAGE) RECORD COMPANY: NORMAL RECORDS ART DIRECTORS: KERSTIN VIEG, OLAF MEYER DESIGNER: OLAF MEYER PHOTOGRAPHER: KERSTIN VIEG PERFORMING ARTIST: COSMIC PSYCHOS ALBUM TITLE: SLAVE TO THE CRAVE

(THIS PAGE) RECORD COMPANY: POLYGRAM RECORDS ART DIRECTOR: SHERYL LUTZ-BROWN DESIGNER: ETSUKO ISEKI ILLUSTRATOR: CRISTIAN CLAYTON PERFORMING ARTISTS: VARIOUS ALBUM TITLE: HARD ROCK ESSENTIALS 1970's & 1980's ■ (OPPOSITE PAGE) RECORD COMPANY: © 1990 WARNER BROS. RECORDS ART DIRECTORS: KIM CHAMPAGNE, JEFF GOLD DESIGNER: KIM CHAMPAGNE ILLUSTRATOR AND LOGO: BARRY JACKSON PHOTOGRAPHERS: WALTAIRE "MOJO PHOTO" BALDWIN, ROBERT "MINT MAN" JOHNSON, MISS "X" TINE DESIGN FIRM: WARNER BROS. IN-HOUSE ART DEPARTMENT PERFORMING ARTIST: ZZ TOP ALBUM TITLE: RECYCLER

RECORD COMPANY: SUB POP
ART DIRECTOR/DESIGNER: ART CHANTRY
PERFORMING ARTIST: LOVE BATTERY
ALBUM TITLE: DAYGLO

RECORD COMPANY: SUB POP
ART DIRECTOR/DESIGNER: ART CHANTRY
PHOTOGRAPHER: ARTHUR S. AUBRY
PERFORMING ARTIST/ALBUM TITLE: PIGEONHED

(ALL IMAGES THIS SPREAD) ART DIRECTOR: ART CHANTRY DESIGNER: ART CHANTRY ■ (THIS PAGE) RECORD COMPANY: AMPHETAMINE REPTILE RECORDS PERFORMING ARTIST: S.W.A.T. ALBUM TITLE: DEEP INSIDE A COP'S MIND ■ (OPPOSITE PAGE) RECORD COMPANY: SUB POP RECORDS PERFORMING ARTIST: MARK LANEGAN ALBUM TITLE: WHISKEY FOR THE HOLY GHOST

(THIS PAGE) RECORD COMPANY: LUCKY RECORDS ART DIRECTOR/DESIGNER: ART CHANTRY PERFORMING ARTIST: THE FASTBACKS ALBUM TITLE:
BIKE, TOY, CLOCK, GIFT ■ (OPPOSITE TOP AND BOTTOM) RECORD COMPANY: CHRYSALIS RECORDS ART DIRECTOR/DESIGNER: EDDIE
DEIGHTON PERFORMING ARTIST: BLONDIE ALBUM TITLE: ATOMIC ■ (OPPOSITE CENTER LEFT) RECORD COMPANY: 3:23 RECKERDS ART DIRECTOR/
DESIGNER: ART CHANTRY PERFORMING ARTIST: VARIOUS ALBUM TITLE: WARM AND FUZZY FEELINGS ■ (OPPOSITE CENTER RIGHT) RECORD
COMPANY: CHUCKIE-BOY RECORDS ART DIRECTOR/DESIGNER: ART CHANTRY PERFORMING ARTIST: THE HOLIDAYS ALBUM TITLE: CHUCKIE-BOY

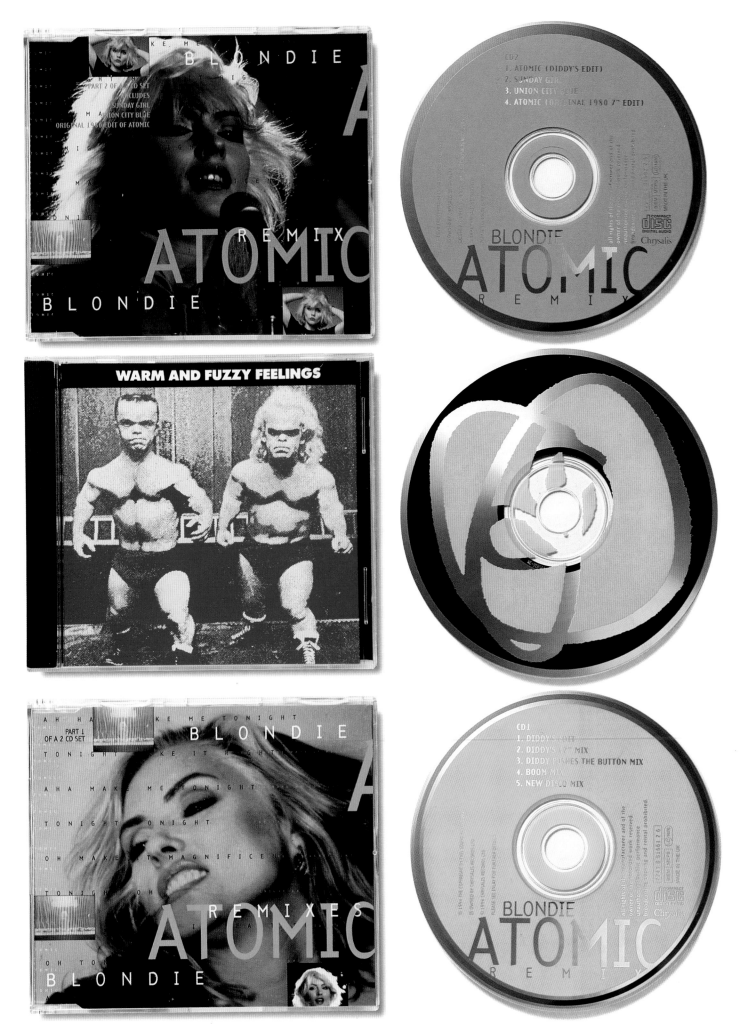

(OPPOSITE) RECORD COMPANY: MERCURY RECORDS ART DIRECTOR: NIKKO AMANDONICO DESIGNER: NIKKO AMANDONICO DESIGN FIRM: ENERGY PROJECT PERFORMING ARTISTS: VARIOUS ALBUM TITLE: POPMUSIC FROM... ■ (THIS PAGE) RECORD COMPANY: SIRE/WARNER BROS.

ART DIRECTORS: SYLVIA REED, SPENCER DRATE DESIGNERS: SYLVIA REED, SPENCER DRATE ADDITIONAL DESIGN: DENNIS ASCIENZO, JÜTKA SALAVETZ PHOTOGRAPHER: LOUIS JAMMES DESIGN FIRM: JUSTDESIGN PERFORMING ARTIST: LOU REED ALBUM TITLE: MAGIC AND LOSS

(THIS PAGE) RECORD COMPANY: VIRGIN RECORDS U.K. ART DIRECTOR/DESIGNER: NORMAN MOORE PHOTOGRAPHER: KEN NAHOUM DESIGN FIRM: DESIGN ART INC. PERFORMING ARTIST: BELINDA CARLISLE ALBUM TITLE: VISION OF YOU ■ (OPPOSITE TOP LEFT) RECORD COMPANY: EPIC ART DIRECTOR/DESIGNER: NORMAN MOORE PHOTOGRAPHER: ANDREW CATLIN DESIGN FIRM: DESIGN ART INC. PERFORMING ARTIST: SADE ALBUM TITLE: LOVE DELUXE ■ (OPPOSITE PAGE TOP RIGHT) RECORD COMPANY: CAPITOL RECORDS ART DIRECTOR/DESIGNER: NORMAN

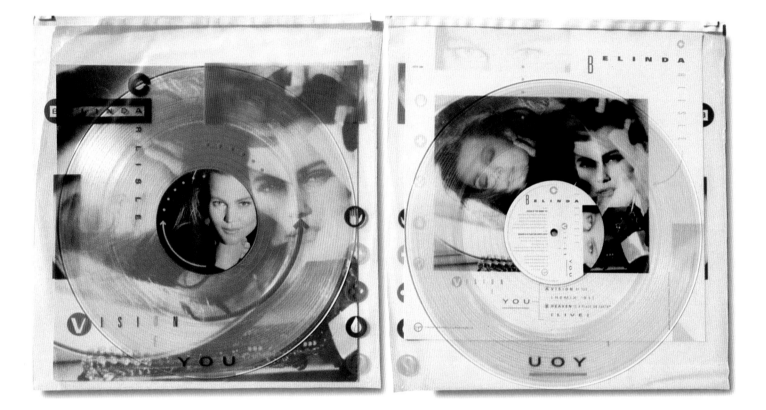

MOORE PHOTOGRAPHER: NORMAN MOORE DESIGN FIRM: DESIGN ART INC. PERFORMING ARTIST: TINA TURNER ALBUM TITLE: SHE HERO: A TRIBUTE TO TINA TURNER ■ (OPPOSITE PAGE BOTTOM LEFT) RECORD COMPANY: A+M RECORDS ART DIRECTOR/DESIGNER/PHOTOGRAPHER: NORMAN MOORE DESIGN FIRM: DESIGN ART INC. PERFORMING ARTISTS: VARIOUS ALBUM TITLE: 38 SPECIAL ROCK AND ROLL STRATEGY ■ (OPPOSITE PAGE BOTTOM RIGHT) RECORD COMPANY: ATLANTIC RECORDS ART DIRECTOR: NORMAN MOORE DESIGNER: NORMAN MOORE PHOTOGRAPHER: DAN WINTERS DESIGN FIRM: DESIGNART INC. PERFORMING ARTIST: BAD RELIGION ALBUM TITLE: STRANGER THAN FICTION

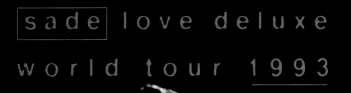

sade love deluxe
world tour 1993

(THIS PAGE) RECORD COMPANY: CAPITOL RECORDS ART DIRECTOR/DESIGNER/PHOTOGRAPHER: NORMAN MOORE DESIGN FIRM: DESIGN ART INC. PERFORMING ARTIST: TINA TURNER ALBUM TITLE: TINA ■ (OPPOSITE TOP) RECORD COMPANY: SPV RECORDS DESIGNER/PHOTOGRAPHER: SABINE POTTHAST PERFORMING ARTISTS: VARIOUS ALBUM TITLE: NIGHTLINE ■ (OPPOSITE SECOND ROW) RECORD COMPANY: SPV RECORDS DESIGNER:

MARIANNE VON ALLESCH PERFORMING ARTIST/ALBUM TITLE: MR. LAWRENCE ■ (OPPOSITE THIRD ROW) RECORD COMPANY: SPV RECORDS DESIGNER: ELKE WEISSE PERFORMING ARTIST: INVISIBLE LIMITS ALBUM TITLE: FAMILIAR ■ (OPPOSITE BOTTOM ROW) RECORD COMPANY: SPV RECORDS DESIGNER: SABINE POTTHAST PHOTOGRAPHER: NIKOLAJ GEORGIEW PERFORMING ARTISTS: VARIOUS ALBUM TITLE: GLAD TO BE GAY

RECORD COMPANY: MCA RECORDS CREATIVE DIRECTOR BOX SET: ALAN DOUGLAS ART DIRECTORS: VARTAN (BOX SET), ADRIAN BOOT (ULTI-
MATE EXPERIENCE), ALAN DOUGLAS, CHRIS GRIFFIN DESIGNERS: JOHN O'BRIEN, ADRIAN BOOT, DAVID COSTA PHOTOGRAPHER: GERED
MANKOWITZ ILLUSTRATORS: GERED MANKOWITZ, DAVID COSTA PERFORMING ARTIST: JIMI HENDRIX TITLE: THE EXPERIENCE COLLECTION

(OPPOSITE PAGE) RECORD COMPANY: BROTHER ENTERTAINMENT ART DIRECTORS: SPENCER DRATE, JÜTKA SALAVETZ DESIGNERS: SPENCER DRATE, JÜTKA SALAVETZ ILLUSTRATOR: ROBERT LYN NELSON DESIGN FIRM: JUSTDESIGN PERFORMING ARTIST: THE BEACH BOYS ALBUM TITLE: SUMMER IN PARADISE ■ (THIS PAGE TOP) RECORD COMPANY: EMI RECORDS CD PACKAGING, CONCEPT & DESIGN: PENTAGRAM

GRAPHIC DESIGN: FARROW, PET SHOP BOYS PERFORMING ARTIST: PET SHOP BOYS ALBUM TITLE: VERY ■ (THIS PAGE CENTER) RECORD COMPANY: EMI RECORDS ART DIRECTION: ADVERTISING DEPARTMENT EMI ELECTROLA GMBH COVER DESIGNER: DORIS GADEBUSCH COVER PAINTING: SEBASTIAN KRÜGER PERFORMING ARTIST: BAP ALBUM TITLE: PIK SIBBE ■ (THIS PAGE BOTTOM) RECORD COMPANY: EMI RECORDS COVER CONCEPT & DESIGN: DORIS GADEBUSCH PHOTOGRAPHER: FRANZ HAMM/AKG PERFORMING ARTIST: PURPLE SCHULZ ALBUM TITLE: HAHA

(THIS PAGE TOP) RECORD COMPANY: EMI RECORDS COVER IDEA & PHOTOGRAPHY: ANTON CORBIJN ARTWORK: MICHAEL • NASH ASSOCIATES PERFORMING ARTIST: HERBERT GRÖNEMEYER ALBUM TITLE: CHAOS ▪ (THIS PAGE BOTTOM) RECORD COMPANY: EMI RECORDS ART DIRECTION: ADVERTISING DEPARTMENT EMI ELECTROLA GMBH COVER DESIGN: 2D COVER PHOTO GLOBE AND MAIL: JEFF WASSERMAN PERFORMING ARTIST: SHIFTY SHERIFFS ALBUM TITLE: CANNIBAL ANIMAL ▪ (OPPOSITE TOP LEFT) RECORD COMPANY: EMI RECORDS COVER PAINTING & CONCEPT: LOTSI COVER REALISATION: SO.WIE?SO! PERFORMING ARTIST: THROW THAT BEAT IN THE GARBAGE CAN ALBUM TITLE: SUPERSTAR ▪ (OPPOSITE TOP RIGHT) RECORD COMPANY: EMI RECORDS COVER PAINTING: MANFRED "SCHMAL" BOECKER COVER DESIGN: ADAM BACKHAUSEN PERFORMING ARTIST: BAP ALBUM TITLE: DA CAPO ▪ (OPPOSITE BOTTOM LEFT) RECORD COMPANY: EMI RECORDS ART DIRECTION: ADVERTISING DEPARTMENT, EMI ELECTROLA GMBH COVER DESIGN: NENO! PHOTOGRAPHER: MARTIN BECKER PERFORMING ARTIST: BRINGS ALBUM TITLE: HEX 'N' SEX ▪ (OPPOSITE BOTTOM RIGHT) RECORD COMPANY: EMI RECORDS ART DIRECTOR: ADVERTISING DEPARTMENT, EMI ELECTROLA GMBH COVER DESIGN: CCG PERFORMING ARTIST: FATS DOMINO ALBUM TITLE: DANCE WITH MR. DOMINO

RECORD COMPANY: CHRYSALIS RECORDS
ART DIRECTORS: ANDREW GREETHMAN, CARTER USM
DESIGNER: ANDREW GREETHMAN
PERFORMING ARTIST: CARTER USM
ALBUM TITLE: POST HISTORIC MONSTERS

RECORD COMPANY: NORMAL RECORDS
ART DIRECTORS: KERSTIN VIEG, OLAF MEYER
DESIGNER: OLAF MEYER
PHOTOGRAPHER: KERSTIN VIEG
PERFORMING ARTIST: TERRY LEE HALE
ALBUM TITLE: OH WHAT A WORLD

(THIS PAGE) ■ RECORD COMPANY: CASTLE VON BUHLER STUDIOS ART DIRECTOR: FRITZ KLAETKE DESIGNER: FRITZ KLAETKE PHOTOGRAPHER: WILLIAM HUBER DESIGN FIRM: VISUAL DIALOGUE PERFORMING ARTISTS: VARIOUS ALBUM TITLE: SOON ■ (OPPOSITE TOP) RECORD COMPANY: ATLANTIC RECORDS ART DIRECTOR: MELANIE NISSEN PHOTOGRAPHER: MELANIE NISSEN DESIGNERS: MELANIE NISSEN, SUNG LEE, CHARLIE BECKER PERFORMING ARTIST: JOE HENRY ALBUM TITLE: KINDNESS OF THE WORLD ■ (OPPOSITE CENTER) RECORD COMPANY: RECREC MUSIC ART DIRECTOR/ILLUSTRATOR: ANDREA CAPREZ DESIGNER: ROLAND FISCHBACHER PERFORMING ARTIST: JELLY-FISH KISS ALBUM TITLE: LUNA HOTEL ■ (OPPOSITE BOTTOM) RECORD COMPANY: WORD RECORDS ART DIRECTOR: DIANA BARNES DESIGNERS: JEFF FRANKE, LISA FRANKE PHOTOGRAPHER: MATTHEW BARNES DESIGN FIRM: FRANKE DESIGN PERFORMING ARTIST: RANDY STONEHILL ALBUM TITLE: STORIES ■ (FOLLOWING SPREAD LEFT) RECORD COMPANY: ROUGH TRADE RECORDS ART DIRECTOR/PHOTOGRAPHER: FRITZ BRINCKMANN TYPOGRAPHER: PHILIP VON WINTERFELDT IMAGE TREATMENT: PIT BEYER DESIGN FIRM: HERZ° HAMBURG PERFORMING ARTISTS: EINSTÜRZENDE NEUBAUTEN

ALBUM TITLES: TABULA RASA, MALEDICTION, INTERIM ■ (FOLLOWING SPREAD RIGHT TOP LEFT) RECORD COMPANY: © 1992 SIRE RECORDS ART DIRECTOR: JERI HEIDEN DESIGNERS: JERI HEIDEN, GREG ROSS PHOTOGRAPHER: GLEN ERLER PERFORMING ARTIST: K.D. LANG ALBUM TITLE: INGÉNUE ■ (FOLLOWING SPREAD RIGHT TOP RIGHT) RECORD COMPANY: CAPITOL RECORDS ART DIRECTORS: TOMMY STEELE, JEFFERY FEY DESIGNER: JEFFERY FEY LOGO/LETTERING: MARGO CHASE PHOTOGRAPHER: MERLYN ROSENBERG PERFORMING ARTIST: BONNIE RAITT ALBUM TITLE: LUCK OF THE DRAW ■ (FOLLOWING SPREAD RIGHT PAGE CENTER) RECORD COMPANY: ATLANTIC RECORDS ART DIRECTOR: RICHARD BATES DESIGNERS: RICHARD BATES, SUNG LEE PHOTOGRAPHER: GLEN ERLER PERFORMING ARTIST: MELISSA FERRICK ALBUM TITLE: MASSIVE BLUR ■ (FOLLOWING SPREAD RIGHT PAGE BOTTOM LEFT) RECORD COMPANY: SONY MUSIC ART DIRECTOR: CHRISTOPHER AUSTOPCHUK DESIGNER: TRACEY BOYCHUK PHOTOGRAPHER: ANDREW ECCLES PERFORMING ARTIST: YOUSS OU N'DOUR ALBUM TITLE: THE GUIDE (WOMMAT) ■ (FOLLOWING SPREAD RIGHT PAGE BOTTOM RIGHT) RECORD COMPANY: EPIC/SONY MUSIC ART DIRECTOR: SARA ROTMAN DESIGNER: SARA ROTMAN PERFORMING ARTIST: THE THE ALBUM TITLE: LOVE IS STRONGER THAN DEATH

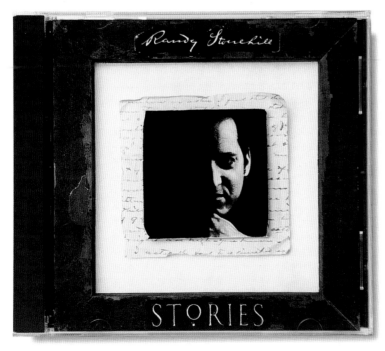
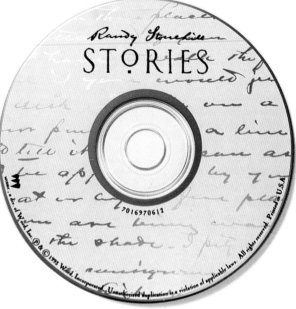

(THIS PAGE) RECORD COMPANY: FLYSUPE PRODUCTIONS ART DIRECTOR/DESIGNER: JOHN SAYLES ILLUSTRATOR: JOHN SAYLES DESIGN FIRM: SAYLES GRAPHIC DESIGN PERFORMING ARTIST: THE FLYING MARSUPIALS ALBUM TITLE: WORKING WITHOUT ANNETTE ■ (OPPOSITE TOP LEFT) RECORD COMPANY: POLYGRAM RECORDS ART DIRECTION: GÜNTER WOLF, BEST OF... DESIGN: VOLKER NEUMANN, Z-ART COVER CONCEPT: STEVE HAHN PHOTOGRAPHER: MARTIN BECKER PERFORMING ARTIST: JINGO DE LUNCH ALBUM TITLE: DEJA VOODOO ■ (OPPOSITE

TOP RIGHT AND CENTER) RECORD COMPANY: POLYGRAM RECORDS COVER LOGO: EMBROIDERY EXPRESS PERFORMING ARTIST: THE ALLMAN BROTHERS BAND ALBUM TITLE: A DECADE OF HITS 1969–1979 ■ (OPPOSITE PAGE BOTTOM LEFT) RECORD COMPANY: POLYGRAM RECORDS ART DIRECTOR: MICHAEL SOWA DESIGNER: RYAN ART PHOTOGRAPHER: LAWRENCE WATSON PERFORMING ARTIST: MIAOW ALBUM TITLE: THE BEAUTIFUL SOUTH ■ (OPPOSITE PAGE BOTTOM RIGHT) RECORD COMPANY: POLYGRAM RECORDS ART DIRECTOR/DESIGNER: DIRK RUDOLPH PHOTOGRAPHERS: DIRK RUDOLPH, HOLGER GROSS PERFORMING ARTIST: ELEMENT OF CRIME ALBUM TITLE: AN EINEM SONNTAG IM APRIL

THE ALLMAN BROTHERS BAND
a decade of hits 1969-1979

AAD

COMPACT
disc
DIGITAL AUDIO

314 511 156-2

Polydor

1. STATESBORO BLUES • 2. RAMBLIN' MAN
3. MIDNIGHT RIDER • 4. SOUTHBOUND • 5. MELISSA
6. JESSICA • 7. AIN'T WASTIN' TIME NO MORE
8. LITTLE MARTHA • 9. CRAZY LOVE • 10. REVIVAL
11. WASTED WORDS • 12. BLUE SKY • 13. ONE WAY OUT
14. IN MEMORY OF ELIZABETH REED
15. DREAMS • 16. WHIPPING POST

FL02

THE BEAUTIFUL SOUTH

MIAOW

ELEMENT of CriME
an einem Sonntag im April

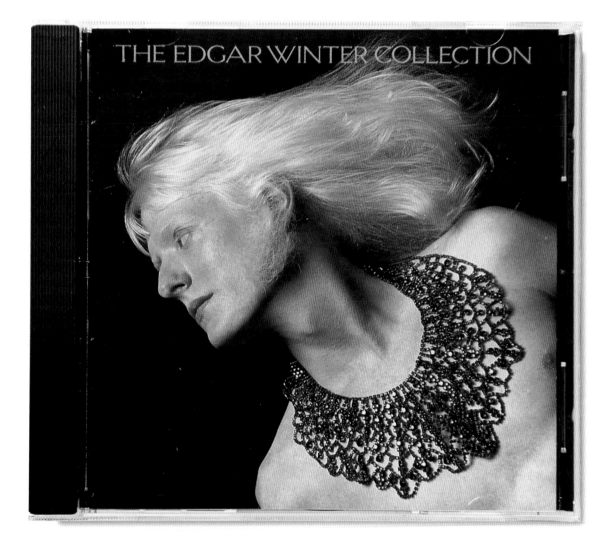

(OPPOSITE PAGE) RECORD COMPANY: LEGACY RECORDS ART DIRECTOR: NICKY LINDEMAN PERFORMING ARTIST: JEFF BECK ALBUM TITLE: BECKOLOGY ■ (THIS PAGE) RECORD COMPANY: RHINO RECORDS ART DIRECTOR: GEOFF GANS DESIGNER: ROSA SCHUTH PHOTOGRAPHER: FRANCESCO SCAVULLO PERFORMING ARTIST: EDGAR WINTER ALBUM TITLE: THE EDGAR WINTER COLLECTION

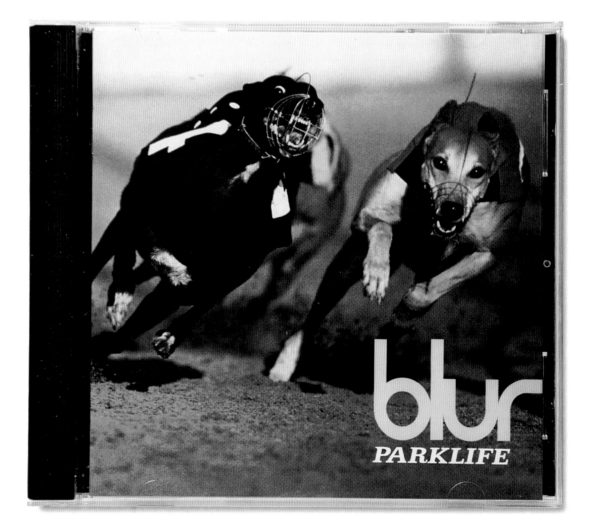

(ABOVE AND OPPOSITE TOP) RECORD COMPANY: SBK RECORDS DESIGN FIRM: STYRLOROUGE PHOTOGRAPHER: BRUNSKILL/BOB THOMAS PERFORM-
ING ARTIST: BLUR ALBUM TITLE: PARKLIFE ■ (OPPOSITE BOTTOM) RECORD COMPANY: MCA RECORDS ART DIRECTOR: VARTAN DESIGNERS: TAKI
ONO, AYAKO NAGANO ILLUSTRATOR: TADANORI YOKOO PERFORMING ARTISTS: JOHN CALE, BOB NEUWIRTH ALBUM TITLE: LAST DAY ON EARTH

(THIS PAGE) RECORD COMPANY: © 1993 SIRE RECORDS ART DIRECTORS: KIM CHAMPAGNE, JEFF GOLD PACKAGE CONCEPT AND DESIGN: PAUL WESTERBERG, KIM CHAMPAGNE BOOK DESIGNERS: KIM CHAMPAGNE, JEAN KRIKORIAN DESIGN FIRM: WARNER BROS. IN-HOUSE ART

DEPARTMENT PERFORMING ARTIST: PAUL WESTERBERG ALBUM TITLE: 14 SONGS ■ (OPPOSITE) RECORD COMPANY: WARNER BROS. RECORDS ART DIRECTOR/DESIGNER: PAUL ELLEDGE ILLUSTRATOR/PHOTOGRAPHER: PAUL ELLEDGE PERFORMING ARTIST: MINISTRY ALBUM TITLE: PSALM 69

ΚΕΦΑΛΗΞΘ

N.W.O 5:29
Just one Fix 5:11
TV Ⅱ 3:04
Hero 4:12
Jesus Built my Hotrod 4:51
Scarecrow 8:21
Psalm 69 5:29
Corrosion 4:55
Grace 3:06

Produced By
H. Luxa/H. Pan for Luxa/Pan Productions

Ministry:

A. Jourgensen: Vox, Gtrs, Kbds.
P. Barker: Bass. Programming. Vox

Additional Personnel:

W. Rieflin: Drums
M. Scaccia: Gtr
M. Balch: Kbds. Programming.
H. Beno: Programming
L. Svitek: Gtr.

Also:
G. Haynes * Vox and Lyrics (J.B.M.H.R.)

SPV 055-93773 Made in Austria by DADC

RECORD COMPANY: SPV RECORDS
DESIGNER: SABINE POTTHAST
PERFORMING ARTIST: PLASTIC BERTRAND
ALBUM TITLE: CA PLANE POUR MOI

INDEX

VERZEICHNIS

INDEX

PHOTOGRAPHERS·ILLUSTRATORS·ARTISTS

DESIGN FIRMS

RECORD COMPANIES

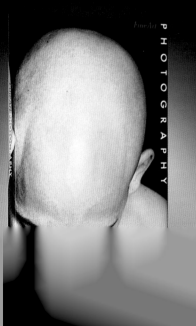

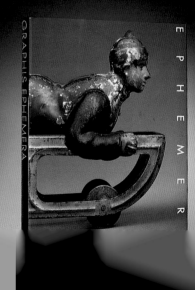

G R A P H I S B O O K S

Graphis 296

Graphis 296

The Digital Revolution: BVGA Scitimage Silicon Graphics European Mindscapes Multimedia

Graphis 295

Graphis 295

Carson Chiat/Day Apeloig Leith Agosey Leigoriella Gorham

Graphis 297

Graphis 297

Knoma Fletcher Arndt AIIV Achilli & Piazza CD Boxed Sets

G R A P H I S M A G A Z I N E